zoom
Deutsch 1

Higher
Workbook

Oliver Gray

OXFORD

Great Clarendon Street, Oxford OX2 6DP

Oxford University Press is a department of the University of Oxford.

It furthers the University's objective of excellence in research, scholarship, and education by publishing worldwide in
Oxford New York Auckland Cape Town Dar es Salaam Hong Kong Karachi
Kuala Lumpur Madrid Melbourne Mexico City Nairobi New Delhi Shanghai
Taipei Toronto

With offices in
Argentina Austria Brazil Chile Czech Republic France Greece Guatemala
Hungary Italy Japan South Korea Poland Portugal Singapore Switzerland
Thailand Turkey Ukraine Vietnam

Oxford is a registered trade mark of Oxford University Press
in the UK and in certain other countries

British Library Cataloguing in Publication Data

Data available

ISBN 978 019 9127726

24

Printed in Great Britain by Bell and Bain Ltd, Glasgow

The manufacturing process conforms to the environmental
regulations of the country of origin.

Acknowledgements

The author and publisher would like to thank the following people for their help and advice: Michael Spencer (editor), Angelika Libera (language consultant).

Audio recordings by Boris Steinberg at Slomophone Audio Studio, Berlin

The author and publisher would like to thank the following for their permission to reproduce photographs and other copyright material:

Cover: The Ampelmann is a registered trademark of AMPELMANN GmbH Berlin, www.ampelmann.de

P8tl: Jonathan Larsen/Shutterstock; p8tr: INTERFOTO/Alamy; p8m: OUP; p9l: Nikola Spasenoski/Shutterstock; p9m: Kuttelvaserova/Shutterstock; p9m: Morgan Lane Photography/Shutterstock; p9m: Guy Shapira/Shutterstock; p9m: Monkey Business Images/ Shutterstock; p9r: @erics/Shutterstock; p12: Map Resources/Shutterstock; p16: OUP; p26: OUP; p33: OUP; p72: Elena Aliaga/Shutterstock; p73: Santje/Shutterstock; p74: Bob Cheung/ Shutterstock; p75m: Romeo Huidu/Shutterstock; p74b: Pavol Kmeto/Shutterstock.

Illustrations by: Matt Ward, Tim Kahane, Matt Latchford, Stefan Chabluk, James Stayte.

Every effort has been made to contact copyright holders of material reproduced in this book. If notified, the publishers will be pleased to rectify any errors or omissions at the earliest opportunity.

Inhalt

Pronunciation overview   4

Einheit 0: Hallo!

0.1	Wie heißt du?	8
0.2	Wie alt bist du?	9
0.3	Ich habe Geburtstag!	10
0.4	Mein Land, meine Sprache	11
0.5	Kathis Videoblog	12
0.6a	Sprachlabor	13
0.6b	Think	14
0	Vokabular	15

Einheit 1A: Meine Familie

1A.1	Das ist meine Familie!	16
1A.2	Ich habe einen Bruder	17
1A.3	Hast du ein Haustier?	18
1A.4	Wie bist du?	19
1A.5	Nicos Videoblog	20
1A.6a	Sprachlabor	21
1A.6b	Think	22
1A	Vokabular	23

Einheit 1B: Meine Schule

1B.1	Mein Klassenzimmer	24
1B.2	Schulfächer	25
1B.3	Wie spät ist es?	26
1B.4	Mein Schultag	27
1B.5	Ninas Videoblog	28
1B.6a	Sprachlabor	29
1B.6b	Think	30
1B	Vokabular	31

Einheit 2A: Freizeit und Hobbys

2A.1	Ich spiele gern Fußball	32
2A.2	Das mache ich am liebsten	33
2A.3	Ich liebe Computerspiele	34
2A.4	Wie oft machst du das?	35
2A.5	Am Wochenende	36
2A.6a	Sprachlabor	37
2A.6b	Think	38
2A	Vokabular	39

Einheit 2B: Wo wohnst du?

2B.1	Meine Region	40
2B.2	Hier wohne ich	41
2B.3	Mein Haus	42
2B.4	Mein Zimmer	43
2B.5	Kathis Videoblog	44
2B.6a	Sprachlabor	45
2B.6b	Think	46
2B	Vokabular	47

Einheit 3A: Guten Appetit!

3A.1	Was isst du gern?	48
3A.2	Ein Eis, bitte!	49
3A.3	500 Gramm Käse, bitte!	50
3A.4	Ich esse kein Fleisch	51
3A.5	Nicos Videoblog	52
3A.6a	Sprachlabor	53
3A.6b	Think	54
3A	Vokabular	55

Einheit 3B: Mein Zuhause

3B.1	Berlin, Berlin!	56
3B.2	Was kann man machen?	57
3B.3	Wo ist das Kino?	58
3B.4	Im Zoo	59
3B.5	Besuchen Sie Zoomsdorf!	60
3B.6a	Sprachlabor	61
3B.6b	Think	62
3B	Vokabular	63

Einheit 4A: Modestadt Berlin!

4A.1	Die Jeans ist cool!	64
4A.2	Coole Outfits	65
4A.3	Wir gehen einkaufen!	66
4A.4	Die Hose ist zu klein!	67
4A.5	Das trage ich!	68
4A.6a	Sprachlabor	69
4A.6b	Think	70
4A	Vokabular	71

Einheit 4B: Zu Besuch

4B.1	Die Ferien	72
4B.2	Wir fahren nach Wien!	73
4B.3	Was hast du gemacht?	74
4B.4	Im Prater	75
4B.5	Nicos Videoblog	76
4B.6a	Sprachlabor	77
4B.6b	Think	78
4B	Vokabular	79

Mein Vokabular   80

Pronunciation

Sound German!

German letters are not always pronounced like English ones, but the good news is that once you have learnt how to pronounce German, you will always get it right. This isn't true for all languages.

Consonants

Many German consonants are pronounced the same way as in English. Here are some examples:

 Consonants / Konsonanten

b	Berlin
d	Deutsch
f	Fisch
h	Haus
k	klein
l	lustig
m	Mutter
n	nein
p	Polen
t	Timo

Now here are those which sound different:

 g is never pronounced like the English 'soft g' (as in the words 'George', 'general' and 'age'). It is always 'hard', as in 'ground', 'gap' or 'gun'.

 g / g

grün
Giraffe
Morgen

 j is pronounced like the English 'y'.

 j / j

Joghurt
Jahr
jetzt

 r is the reason some people call the German language 'guttural'. It's quite a gritty sound and needs practising because no sound in English is quite like it.

 r / r

rot
Rhein
Regen
Trier
tragen

 s is pronounced in various ways: – like an English 'z';

 s / s

sieben
sechs
singen

 – like 'sh';

 st – sp / st – sp

Straße
Sturm
spielen

 – like an English 's'.

 s / s

lustig
Maske
fast

Berliner Bär

Pronunciation

v   *v* is pronounced like the English 'f'.

🎧 **v / v**

viel
Vater
vierzig
Vogel
verboten

w   *w* is pronounced like the English 'v'.

🎧 **w / w**

will
Löwe
weiß
Wolke

> You can remember *v* and *w* simply by thinking of the word *Volkswagen* (pronounced in the German way, of course).

q · y   *q* and *y* are hardly used at all, so don't worry about them!

z   'z' is unusual in English (which is why it's worth ten points in Scrabble!). In German, *z* is very common. It is pronounced like the English 'ts'.

🎧 **z / z**

Zoo
Zeit
Zeitung
Zürich

ß   *ß* is the only German letter that doesn't exist in the English alphabet. It represents a double *s* when used after a 'long' vowel (see below).

🎧 **ß / ß**

Straße
groß
Fuß

ss   After a 'short' vowel, *ss* is used instead. It sounds exactly the same.

🎧 **ss / ss**

muss
Schluss
lass
Schloss

Combinations of consonants

ch   The combination of *c* and *h* sounds similar to the 'ch' at the end of the Scottish word 'Loch'.

🎧 **ch / ch**

acht
Achtung
lachen
Loch

sch   The 'sh' sound is extremely common in German but it is spelt *sch*.

🎧 **sch / sch**

schade
Fisch
Schule

Achtung! Acht
Mädchen lachen!

Pronunciation

Vowels

 The letter *a* can be pronounced as a 'short' vowel or as a 'long' vowel.

The short *a* is pronounced like this:

🎧 **Vowels / Vokale**
short a / kurzes a

hat
machen
kann
Mann
Klasse

> Note that it isn't pronounced exactly like an English 'a' as in when we say 'hat'. It's a little bit like a cross between an 'a' and a 'u', as in the English 'hut'. Listen again to check that.

Long *a* – this sounds like the combination 'ar' in English words like 'car':

🎧 **long a / langes a**

Straße
baden
haben
malen

Mmm, Pommes mit Ketchup!

 The short *e* is pronounced like the English 'e', as in 'elephant'. It is never pronounced like the other English 'e', as in 'me'.

🎧 **short e / kurzes e**

England
essen
frech

There is also a long *e*.

🎧 **long e / langes e**

Esel
sehen
leben

 The letter *i* is always pronounced short, as in the English 'in'.

🎧 **i / i**

in
Interview
billig
ich

 The short *o* is pronounced like this:

🎧 **short o / kurzes o**

toll
doppel
Pommes

The long *o* is pronounced like this:

🎧 **long o / langes o**

Mode
Cola
Hallo

Pronunciation

 The short *u* is pronounced like this:

🎧 **short u / kurzes u**

Hund
muss
lustig

The long *u* is pronounced like this:

🎧 **long u / langes u**

Stuhl
Schule
Buch

Combinations of vowels

When two vowels are used together, they make a different sound. This is very common in German.

 ie is pronounced as in the English word 'keep'.

🎧 **ie / ie**

viel
Liebe
sie
vier

 ei is pronounced as in the English word 'eye'.

🎧 **ei / ei**

mein
dein
kein
heiße

 au is pronounced as in the English word 'cow'.

🎧 **au / au**

Haus
Maus
blau

Umlauts

An umlaut is a little symbol that changes the sound of an *a*, *o* or *u*.

Listen to the difference the umlauts make to the sound of each letter.

🎧 **a ⟶ ä**

Vater / Väter
hatte / hätte
Hand / Hände

🎧 **o ⟶ ö**

Post / hören
rot / Löwe
schon / schön

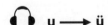

🎧 **u ⟶ ü**

muss / müssen
Gruß / grüßen
pur / für

Eine Maus in einem Haus!

0.1 Wie heißt du?

1 🎧 **Listen to some German names being spelled out. Write down the names.**

a   _Katja_

b   _____

c   _____

d   _____

e   _____

f   _____

g   _____   _____

h   _____   _____

i   _____   _____

j   _____   _____

2 **How do you say these things in German? Write them in and say them out loud.**

a   Say 'Good morning' to someone.

    Guten Morgen!

b   Ask how to write that.

    _____

c   Ask what someone's name is.

    _____

d   Say 'Good evening' to someone.

    _____

e   Say what your name is.

    _____

f   Say 'Goodbye'.

    _____

3 **Say these English words out loud. What German letters do they represent?**

a   HA!   _____

b   BAY   _____

c   CAR   _____

d   SAY   _____

e   YACHT   _____

f   DAY   _____

> Have some fun by trying to write out words for other German letters in this way. Show them to a partner and see if they can identify the letters.

0.2 Wie alt bist du?

1 🎧 **Listen to these people giving you their ages. Write the ages in the bubbles.**

a: 18 b: c: d: e: f:

2 **Add the prices to the labels.**

a: 2,00 €
b:
c:
d:
e:
f:

Hamburger – drei Euro zehn

Schokolade – zwei Euro zwanzig

Bananen – zwei Euro

CD – sechzehn Euro fünfzehn

Lampe – vierzehn Euro

Cola – ein Euro fünfzehn

3 **These people are giving their ages. Write down what they are saying.**

a Ich bin elf Jahre alt.

b _____

c _____

d _____

e _____

f _____

a: 11 b: 17 c: 9 d: 19 e: 7 f: 20

zwanzig   neun   neunzehn   sieben   siebzehn   elf

1 **Solve the clues and write in the German names of the months. The highlighted letters spell another month.**

    a The seventh month of the year.
    b A month for Valentines.
    c The month before the month in clue **a**.
    d The month after the month in clue **a**!
    e It sounds like 'my'.
    f A month with a 'Fool's Day'.

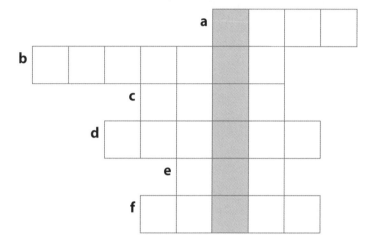

2 **Do the sums, then write the answers, first the number, then the German word. Some words will be left over.**

    a $3 \times 7 =$ ___21___ ___einundzwanzig___

    b $2 \times 15 =$ _____ _____

    c $12 + 12 =$ _____ _____

    d $15 + 12 =$ _____ _____

    e $31 - 9 =$ _____ _____

    f $24 + 4 =$ _____ _____

3 🎧 **Listen and work out how old these people are.**

    a __21__   **c** _____   **e** _____

    b _____   **d** _____   **f** _____

0.4 Mein Land, meine Sprache

1 Find the names of eight countries in this grid. The words can be horizontal, vertical or diagonal.

Write them out below.

_____

_____

_____

_____

_____

_____

_____

_____

G	R	O	B	R	T	N	N	E	N	D	U	E	T
ß	R	Ä	D	E	U	T	S	C	H	L	A	N	D
Ö	P	O	L	E	N	Ü	M	C	O	P	O	L	R
K	N	R	ß	V	B	R	I	F	S	V	U	T	S
A	R	Ä	K	B	F	E	ß	G	T	F	R	K	S
G	B	R	I	T	R	Z	F	B	E	N	G	L	A
ß	P	C	O	R	A	I	Z	F	R	W	S	M	R
A	L	L	E	G	N	D	T	J	R	V	C	I	S
D	E	T	Z	D	K	ß	L	A	E	E	H	Z	P
E	S	Ü	Ü	B	R	V	A	L	N	D	W	Ü	A
Ö	M	R	P	K	E	F	M	S	I	N	E	R	N
S	E	K	R	M	I	L	D	H	S	T	I	C	I
E	B	E	Ä	H	C	H	S	H	C	H	Z	E	E
T	Ü	I	R	K	H	Ö	G	F	H	A	B	H	N

2 Unjumble the countries and insert the language.

a Ich komme aus (tslDhcuaend) _Deutschland_ . Ich spreche _____ .

b Ich komme aus (seÖrictreh) _____ .

Ich spreche _____ .

c Ich komme aus (khainecrrF) _____ .

Ich spreche _____ .

d Ich komme aus (lenoP) _____ . Ich spreche _____ .

e Ich komme aus (pieSnan) _____ .

Ich spreche _____ .

f Ich komme aus (rnßenobiritanG) _____ .

Ich spreche _____ .

3 Write down, in full German sentences:

• what your name is _____

• where you come from _____

• how old you are _____

• when your birthday is _____

• what language(s) you speak _____

0.5 Kathis Videoblog

1 What is the nationality of these people? If you don't recognise any of the town names, look them up.

a   Ich wohne in London. Ich bin _Engländerin_ .

b   Ich wohne in Hamburg. Ich bin _____ .

c   Ich wohne in Innsbruck. Ich bin _____ .

d   Ich wohne in Luzern. Ich bin _____ .

e   Ich wohne in München. Ich bin _____ .

f   Ich wohne in Manchester. Ich bin _____ .

g   Ich wohne in Genf*. Ich bin _____ .

h   Ich wohne in Wien. Ich bin _____ .

* Genf = Geneva

2 🎧 Listen to this girl and circle the correct answers.

a   Anna comes from (Austria) / Germany .

b   She lives in   Seedorf / Seefeld .

c   Her birthday is the first of   March / May .

d   She speaks   German and French / French and Spanish .

e   She thinks French is   great / not so good .

f   She thinks English is   great / not so good .

3 Write a paragraph about yourself.
Mention:

• your name

• where you live

• when your birthday is

• what languages you speak

• what you think of them

_____

_____

_____

_____

_____

_____

_____

_____

1 Translate these countries and languages into German and write the German words in the correct column.

Country	Language
Italien	Italienisch
_____	_____
_____	_____
_____	_____
_____	_____
_____	_____
_____	_____
_____	

> Italian   English   Spain   Turkey   Poland   German   Polish   Italy
> Switzerland   Germany   French   France   Britain   Turkish   Spanish

> One of the countries has three languages. Put that one last.

2 🎧 Using your knowledge of German pronunciation, say these German words out loud. Then check the recording to see how accurate you were.

> ich   Wien   zwei   zwölf   schlecht   dreißig
> Frankreich   Tschüs   wie   Griechenland   fünf

sein (to be) and *haben* (to have)

3 Translate these sentences into German, using the correct form of *haben* or *sein*. Don't translate each word individually, otherwise it won't be correct.

a When is your birthday?   _Wann hast du Geburtstag?_

b My birthday is in December.   _____

c How old are you?   _____

d I am 12 years old.   _____

e Is your birthday in January?   _____

f No, my birthday is in December!   _____

Numbers in German

German numbers over 20 are different from English numbers because the second number comes first. For example, 'twenty-three' is *dreiundzwanzig*, so the first thing you hear is the three.

Be aware of this when you are asking about important numbers such as train times, telephone numbers etc. Try to get in the habit of noting the second number first, so you don't end up missing your train.

1 Take turns to dictate numbers between 20 and 30 to a partner. If you want to hear them again, say *'Wie, bitte?'*. Try to become expert in getting it right first time, because in real life you'll probably only hear each number once.

ei and *ie*

The pronunciation and spelling of *ei* and *ie* is probably the most common error made by learners of German.

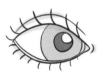

Look at the pictures: *ei* is pronounced like the English word 'eye'; *ie* is pronounced 'eee'. Keep them in mind when listening to and speaking German.

EI　　　　**IE**

2 Read these words aloud and get a partner to write them down accurately:

> Wien　zwei　drei　wie　dreißig　Frankreich　zweiunddreißig
> viel　Griechenland　mein　sieben　heißt　vier

Keeping a vocabulary list

It's a good idea to have a notebook with a separate page for each letter of the alphabet where you can jot down any new words you come across. Remember to note the gender of each noun (*der, die, das*) and to put a capital letter on each. If you have room, you could also keep verbs, nouns, adjectives and adverbs separate.

Learning vocabulary

There are lots of different ways to learn vocabulary. Try some of these out and see which works best for you:
- make a mind map of all the words which relate to a particular topic
- draw pictures next to words in your vocabulary list to help you remember them
- make connections with similar words in English, e.g. *elf* (11) and 'elf'.

0 Vokabular

1 bis 31	1 to 31
eins, zwei, drei	one, two, three
vier, fünf, sechs	four, five, six
sieben, acht, neun	seven, eight, nine
zehn, elf, zwölf	ten, eleven, twelve
dreizehn	thirteen
vierzehn	fourteen
fünfzehn	fifteen
sechzehn	sixteen
siebzehn	seventeen
achtzehn	eighteen
neunzehn	nineteen
zwanzig	twenty
einundzwanzig	twenty-one
zweiundzwanzig	twenty-two
dreiundzwanzig	twenty-three
vierundzwanzig	twenty-four
fünfundzwanzig	twenty-five
sechsundzwanzig	twenty-six
siebenundzwanzig	twenty-seven
achtundzwanzig	twenty-eight
neunundzwanzig	twenty-nine
dreißig	thirty
einunddreißig	thirty-one

Wie alt bist du?	How old are you?
Ich bin … Jahre alt.	I am … years old.
Ich habe am … Geburtstag.	My birthday is on the …
Ich habe im … Geburtstag.	My birthday is in …
Wann hast du Geburtstag?	When is your birthday?
am ersten/zweiten/dritten/ vierten	on the first/second/third/fourth
am zwanzigsten	on the twentieth

Monate	Months
Januar	January
Februar	February
März	March
April	April
Mai	May
Juni	June
Juli	July
August	August
September	September
Oktober	October
November	November
Dezember	December

Wie geht's?	How are you?
Mir geht's gut	I feel good, I'm well
sehr gut	very good
fantastisch	fantastic
nicht so gut	not so good
schlecht	bad

Hallo	Hello
Guten Tag	Hello/Good day
Guten Morgen	Good morning
Guten Abend	Good evening
Auf Wiedersehen	Goodbye
Tschüs	Bye

Wie heißt du?	What's your name?
Ich heiße …	My name is/I am called …
Wie schreibt man das?	How do you spell that?
Das schreibt man …	That is spelled …

Länder	Countries
Ich komme aus …	I come from … (+ country)
Ich wohne in …	I live in … (+ country)
Deutschland	Germany
die Schweiz	Switzerland
die Türkei	Turkey
Frankreich	France
Österreich	Austria
Polen	Poland
Spanien	Spain

Sprachen	Languages
Ich spreche …	I speak … (+ language)
Deutsch	German
Englisch	English
Französisch	French
Italienisch	Italian
Spanisch	Spanish

Checklist

How well do you think you can do the following? Write a sentence for each one if you can.	I can do this well	I can do this but not very well	I can't do this yet
1 say your name, age and when your birthday is			
2 use the German alphabet			
3 pronounce the letters ä, ö, ü, ß, w and ch correctly			
4 count from 1–31			
5 use the verbs haben and sein in the ich and du forms			
6 name a few countries and languages			

1 Who are these relatives? Fill in the gaps with a German word.

a Mehmet ist mein ____Vater____ .

b Suzan ist meine _____ .

c Ayse ist meine _____ .

d Hassan ist mein _____ .

e Ahmed ist mein _____ .

f Rafat ist meine _____ .

2 🎧 Listen to Sascha describing his family. Who is who?

Mein Vater heißt ____B____ .   Meine Schwester heißt _____ .

Meine Mutter heißt _____ .   Mein Bruder heißt _____ .

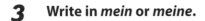

Klaus   Maria   Susanne   Boris

3 Write in *mein* or *meine*.

a __mein__ Bruder

b _____ Schwester

c _____ Oma

d _____ Vater

e _____ Opa

f _____ Großeltern

g _____ Mutter

1 Write in the words for these relatives.

a

c

e

b

d

f

a Ich habe ___einen___ ___Bruder___ .

b Ich habe _____ _____ .

c Ich habe _____ _____ .

d Ich habe _____ _____ .

e Ich bin _____ .

f Ich habe _____ _____ _____ _____ _____ .

> eine Schwester
> einen Bruder
> zwei Schwestern
> zwei Brüder
> Einzelkind

2 🎧 Listen to these people (a–f). How many brothers and sisters do they have? Write the answers in English.

a ___two sisters___

b _____

c _____

d _____

e _____

f _____

3 Translate these sentences.

a I've got two brothers.   ___Ich habe___ _____

b I've got one sister.   _____

c I've got two sisters.   _____

d I've got one brother.   _____

e I've got three brothers.   _____

f I've got no brothers or sisters.   _____

1 **Describe these animals.**

a  brown

c  grey

e  white

b  black

d  brown and white

f  yellow

a Das ist ein ___Pferd___ . Es ist _____ .

b Das ist ein _____ . Er ist _____ .

c Das ist eine _____ . Sie ist _____ .

d Das ist eine _____ . Sie ist _____ und _____ .

e Das ist eine _____ . Sie ist _____ .

f Das ist ein _____ . Er ist _____ .

2 **Listen to these people. What pets do they have? Write the answers in English.**

a ___two cats and___

b _____

c _____

d _____

e _____

f _____

3 **Write in the numbers and the correct plural forms.**

a ___zwei M_____

d  _____

b  _____

e  _____

c _____

f  _____

1 Write in the adjectives. What is the mystery word down?

a

b

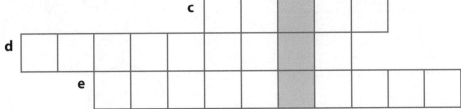

c

d

e

The mystery word down is _____ . It means _____ .

2 Kalle Klug is a cool guy. Which sentences are true and which are false? Write *richtig* (true) or *falsch* (false).

a Kalle ist sehr schüchtern.   _falsch_

b Er ist intelligent.   _____

c Er ist nicht sportlich.   _____

d Er ist ziemlich klein.   _____

e Kalle ist groß.   _____

f Er ist sehr musikalisch.   _____

1A.5 Nicos Videoblog

1 🎧 Listen and answer these questions in English.

Hi! Ich heiße Tim.

a How old is Tim?

Tim is _____

b Where does he live?

_____

c How old is his sister?

_____

d What is she like? Mention two characteristics.

_____

e How old is Tim's brother?

_____

f What is he like? Mention two characteristics.

_____

2 Unjumble the words to make animals. Write out the German word and its English translation.

a E N F L I D _____Delfin_____ , _____dolphin_____

b F A F E _____ , _____

c H A S N O N R _____ , _____

d W Ö L E _____ , _____

e G O L E V _____ , _____

f F E N E L A T _____ , _____

3 Write down these animals and their characteristics in English.

a Ein Delfin ist sportlich, intelligent und fleißig.
b Ein Löwe ist laut, faul und frech.

a _____

b _____

Gender

All nouns are masculine, feminine or neuter:

masculine	ein Fisch	er
feminine	eine Maus	sie
neuter	ein Kaninchen	es

	masculine	feminine	neuter
my	mein Bruder	meine Schwester	mein Pferd
your	dein Onkel	deine Tante	dein Meerschweinchen

Possessive adjectives

1 **Write full sentences like the example provided.**

Example: _Das ist meine Schwester. Sie heißt Paula._

Example:
sister, Paula

a _____

b _____

c _____

d _____

e _____

f _____

a brother, Klaus

d aunt, sporty

b granddad, Helmut

e brown

c Schnurri

f parents

masculine	Ich habe keinen Hamster.
feminine	Ich habe keine Schwester.
neuter	Ich habe kein Meerschweinchen.

Negative

2 **Complete the sentence using _keinen_, _kein_ or _keine_.**

Ich habe k^{einen} H_____, k_____ K_____,

k_____ P_____ und k_____ G_____ .

Umlauts

1 Say these words out loud.
Get a partner to assess how well you have pronounced them.

> **u / ü:** Hund – schüchtern – Mutter – Mütter – grün – müde
> **o / ö:** Opa – Schildkröte – Onkel – Löwe – schon – schön – zwölf – Oma
> **a / ä:** Nashorn – Bär – Vater – Väter – Apfel – Äpfel – Affe

An 'umlaut' is an item of punctuation found in German but not in English. It changes how a vowel is pronounced. Umlauts are only used with u, o and a.

Noun or adjective?

2 Decide whether these words are nouns or adjectives. Write them in the correct column.

Noun	Adjective
Affe	

AFFE
TIGER
NETT
SCHWESTER
BLAU
ROMANTISCH
SCHWARZ
OPA
SCHLANGE
FAUL
EINZELKIND
GRÜN

Nouns are usually easy to identify in German, as they all start with a capital letter, but here it is more difficult, as the words are printed in capitals.

Singular or plural?

3 Use the vocabulary page to work out the plural of these nouns.

Hund, Mutter, Giraffe, Schlange, Bruder, Katze, Papagei, Schwester, Vater

Hunde,

In English, we mainly make a noun plural by adding an –s. It's very different in German, where there are different ways of making plurals.

Dictionary skills

4 Look up these nouns, which you may not know. Write down the meaning and show you understand the gender by writing *der*, *die* or *das*.

das Geld money   ____ Arbeit _____

____ Polizei _____   ____ Auto _____

____ Tür _____   ____ Fenster _____

____ Boot _____   ____ Wald _____

When looking up a noun, the dictionary will tell you whether it is masculine (m), feminine (f) or neuter (n).

5 Find the infinitive and the meaning of these new verbs in the dictionary.

ich laufe laufen , to run   wir bleiben _____, _____

er bringt _____, _____   ich lerne _____, _____

When looking up a verb, the dictionary will show you the infinitive form.

Meine Familie	My family
Wer ist das?	Who's that?
Ist das dein/e (Vater/Mutter)?	Is that your (father/mother)?
Sind das deine (Großeltern)?	Are these your (grandparents)?
Hast du Geschwister?	Do you have siblings?
Das ist mein/e (Bruder/ Schwester).	This is my (brother/sister).
Das sind (meine Brüder).	These are (my brothers).
Ja, ich habe (einen Bruder).	Yes, I have (a brother).
Nein, ich bin Einzelkind.	No, I'm an only child.
Er/sie heißt (Jens/Julia).	He/she is called (Jens/Julia).
ein Bruder(-üder)	a brother
ein Onkel(-)	an uncle
ein Opa(-s)	a granddad
ein Vater(-äter)	a father
eine Familie(-n)	a family
eine Mutter(-ütter)	a mother
eine Oma(-s)	a grandmother
eine Schwester(-n)	a sister
eine Tante(-n)	an aunt
Eltern	parents
Großeltern	grandparents

Haustiere	Pets
ein Fisch(-e)	a fish
ein Hamster(-)	a hamster
ein Huhn(-ühner)	a chicken
ein Hund(-e)	a dog
ein Kaninchen(-)	a rabbit
eine Katze(-n)	a cat
eine Maus(-äuse)	a mouse
ein Meerschweinchen(-)	a guinea pig
ein Pferd(-e)	a horse
eine Schildkröte(-n)	a tortoise
eine Schlange(-n)	a snake
ein Wellensittich(-e)	a budgie

Tiere im Zoo	Zoo animals
ein Affe(-n)	a monkey
ein Bär(-en)	a bear
ein Delfin(-e)	a dolphin
ein Elefant(-en)	an elephant
eine Giraffe(-n)	a giraffe
ein Löwe(-n)	a lion
ein Nashorn(-örner)	a rhino
ein Papagei(-en)	a parrot
ein Tiger(-)	a tiger
ein Vogel(-ögel)	a bird

Wie bist du?	What are you like?
faul	lazy
fleißig	hard-working
frech	naughty
groß	tall, big
intelligent	intelligent
klein	small
laut	loud
musikalisch	musical
nett	nice
romantisch	romantic
schüchtern	shy
sportlich	sporty
gar nicht	not at all
nicht	not
ziemlich	quite
sehr	very

Farben	Colours
blau	blue
braun	brown
gelb	yellow
grau	grey
grün	green
orange	orange
rot	red
schwarz	black
weiß	white

Checklist

How well do you think you can do the following? Write a sentence for each one if you can.	I can do this well	I can do this but not very well	I can't do this yet
1 talk about your family			
2 use the words for 'my' and 'your'			
3 use *Ich habe eine(n)/ keine(n)* …			
4 use plurals			
5 describe yourself, friends, family and pets			
6 use *er/sie/es* correctly			

1   **Fill the gaps with a question word, an article and a noun from the box.**

a   b   c   d   e   f

a   __Wer__ ist das? Das ist _____ _____ .

b   _____ ist das? Das ist _____ _____ .

c   _____ ist das? Das ist _____ _____ .

d   _____ ist das? Das ist _____ _____ .

e   _____ ist das? Das ist _____ _____ .

f   _____ ist das? Das ist _____ _____ .

> wer   was   der   die   das
> Lehrer   Schüler   Schülerin
> Stuhl   Schreibtisch   Tafel

2   🎧 **What do these people have? Put a tick or a cross.**

a   **Katja:**   ☑   ☐

b   **Sven:**   ☐   ☐

c   **Kim:**   ☐   ☐

d   **Fabian:**   ☐   ☐

3   🎧 **Now write out what they say. Listen again to check.**

a   _Ich habe einen _____ aber kein _____

b   _____

c   _____

d   _____

1 Solve the clues, then fill in the crossword with school subjects in German.

Waagerecht (across)

1 a language spoken in Spain
5 adding, subtracting, geometry
6 plants and animals
10 Beethoven, Beatles, Bob Marley
11 Bang!
12 the countries of the world

Senkrecht (down)

1 plenty of exercise
2 all about computers
3 an ancient language
4 a language spoken in Germany
7 all about the past
8 painting and drawing
9 forces, equations, laws

2 🎧 Listen and decide what the subjects are and what the people think of them. Answer in English.

a Janina thinks _____Spanish_____ is _____

  but _____ is _____ .

b Karl thinks _____ is _____

  and _____ is _____ .

c Nicole thinks _____ is _____

  but _____ is _____ .

d Nils thinks _____ is _____

  but _____ is _____ .

1 🎧 **Listen and fill in the gaps in the timetable to show when each lesson starts.**

	Time	Subject (in English)
1		art
2		
3		
4		
5		
6		

2 **Write in the times next to the clocks.**

12:15 _Viertel nach zwölf_____

15:45 _____

06:00 _____

09:15 _____

11:45 _____

16:15 _____

00:00 _____

08:45 _____

> Viertel   vor   nach
> Uhr   Mitternacht
> sechs   zwölf   neun   vier

1B.4 Mein Schultag

1 Find the German words for the days of the week in this grid (across, down or diagonally).

M	I	S	A	M	S	T	A	G	S	O	N
D	O	N	N	I	N	G	S	A	M	P	R
O	R	N	A	T	A	G	O	L	L	A	H
N	M	O	P	T	R	S	T	U	Z	L	A
N	E	I	N	W	D	W	O	C	H	G	N
E	I	N	M	O	N	T	A	G	A	M	D
R	O	T	A	C	H	T	U	T	N	G	S
S	F	R	I	H	E	D	I	A	H	C	O
T	Z	W	E	D	I	E	N	S	T	A	G
A	G	A	S	T	R	F	W	C	H	O	M
G	R	E	A	F	E	I	R	A	G	T	S

_____

_____

_____

_____

_____

_____

2 Unjumble these sentences to say what subjects these people have on which day. Then translate each sentence into English.

a ich Donnerstag Musik Am Mathe habe und

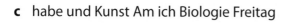
Am Donnerstag habe ich _____

On Thursday I have _____

b Erdkunde Spanisch und Montag ich Am habe

_____

_____

c habe und Kunst Am ich Biologie Freitag

_____

_____

d Am Latein Englisch und ich Dienstag habe

_____

_____

e Mittwoch ich Informatik Am habe Deutsch und

_____

_____

1 🎧 **Listen and fill in the lessons for Thursday and Friday. There may be some double lessons.**

	Montag	Dienstag	Mittwoch	Donnerstag	Freitag
08.45				Informatik	
10.00					
10.45					
11.30					
12.15					
13.00					

2 **Now fill in the timetable in German for Monday, Tuesday and Wednesday using the information below. There may be some double lessons.**

Montag um Viertel vor elf: (Art)

Dienstag um halb zwölf: (German)

Montag um Viertel vor neun: (Religion)

Dienstag um dreizehn Uhr: (French)

Montag um halb zwölf: (Biology)

Dienstag um Viertel vor neun: (Maths)

Mittwoch um Viertel nach zwölf: (English)

Dienstag um Viertel vor elf: (Geography)

Mittwoch um ein Uhr: (English)

Mittwoch um Viertel vor neun: (Italian)

Montag um ein Uhr: (Sport)

Mittwoch um zehn Uhr: (Italian)

Montag um Viertel nach zwölf: (Spanish)

Mittwoch um halb zwölf: (French)

Montag um zehn Uhr: (History)

Mittwoch um Viertel vor elf: (Chemistry)

Dienstag um zehn Uhr: (Maths)

Dienstag um Viertel nach zwölf: (ICT)

3 **Choose five subjects and write down your opinions, using *Ich finde …* and words like *prima*, *langweilig* etc.**

Articles

1   Write in the correct word for 'the' for these words. If you don't know the gender, or can't work it out, look it up.

m = masculine = der
f = feminine = die
n = neuter = das

__der__ Stuhl   _____ Schreibtisch   _____ Klassenzimmer

_____ Lehrer   _____ Lehrerin   _____ Tafel

_____ Heft   _____ Schülerin   _____ Schüler

_____ Direktor   _____ Bibliothek   _____ Schulhof

haben

2   Insert the person and the correct form of *haben* into these sentences:

a   Am Montag __habe__ _____ Mathe. (*I*)

b   Am Freitag _____ _____ Spanisch. (*he*)

c   Am Dienstag _____ _____ Kunst. (*we*)

d   Am Mittwoch _____ _____ Informatik. (*you – singular*)

e   Am Donnerstag _____ _____ Physik. (*we*)

f   Am Montag _____ _____ Sport. (*I*)

ich habe
du hast
er/sie/es hat
wir haben

Word order

3   Write sentences based on the clues. Write each sentence three times, using the *ich* form, the *er* form and the *wir* form.

Remember, the verb comes second.

a   Tuesday

$a^2 + b^2 = c^2$

Am Dienstag habe ich _____

_____

_____

b   Monday

_____

_____

_____

c   Friday

_____

_____

_____

d   Wednesday

_____

_____

_____

Montag

Dienstag

Mittwoch

Freitag

Kunst

Mathe

Informatik

Musik

Recognising words

1 Use the clues to help you find the words.
Write the words in English and German.

Clue		English word	German word
a	A 'pocket reckoner'	calculator	Taschenrechner
b	Something to keep papers in order		
c	Something you sit at when you write		
d	Something you fill with ink		
e	A subject concerning the earth		
f	Like a stool but with a back on it		
g	In the middle of the night		
h	In the middle of the week		
i	A subject that gives you information		
j	Something used for drawing lines		

Ordner   Mittwoch   Lineal   Stuhl   Taschenrechner

Erdkunde   Mitternacht   Informatik   Füller   Schreibtisch

> For the activities on this page, refer to the vocabulary page of your text book.

> German is a good language for guessing the meanings of words because it is a logical language and often combines two or more words into one. In the first example, *Tasche* means 'pocket' and *Rechner* means 'reckoner'. A 'pocket reckoner' is a calculator. With a bit of logical thought and clever guess work, there are lots of words you can understand.

Similar words

2 Circle any word that you can immediately recognise because it is so similar to an English word. If there are any borderline cases, discuss them with others in the class.

Englisch   Deutsch   Stuhl   fantastisch   langweilig

interessant   Kunst   Latein   super   Dienstag   Spanisch

Lieblingsfach   Sport   doof   Mathe   Musik

> You can get off to a good start in understanding German because so many words are similar to English ones.

Ways to pronounce 'o'

3 Translate these words into German, write them down and then say them out loud.

stupid, folder, Monday, sport, Sunday, rhinoceros, religion, wolf

doof,

> This one vowel can be pronounced in various ways.

Mein Klassenzimmer	**My classroom**
das Klassenzimmer	classroom
der Lehrer	teacher (male)
die Lehrerin	teacher (female)
der Schreibtisch	desk
der Schüler	pupil (male)
die Schülerin	pupil (female)
der Stuhl	chair
die Tafel	board, chalkboard

Schulsachen	**School equipment**
der Bleistift	pencil
die Federtasche	pencil case
der Filzstift	felt-tip pen
der Füller	fountain pen
das Heft	exercise book
der Kuli	ballpoint pen
das Lineal	ruler
der Ordner	file
der Radiergummi	eraser
das Schulbuch	school book
die Schultasche	school bag
der Taschenrechner	calculator

Schulfächer	**School subjects**
Deutsch	German
Englisch	English
Erdkunde	geography
Französisch	French
Geschichte	history
Informatik	IT
Kochen	cookery
Kunst	art
Latein	Latin
Mathe	maths
Medienwissenschaften	media studies
Naturwissenschaften (Biologie, Chemie, Physik)	sciences (biology, chemistry, physics)
Religion	religion, RE
Spanisch	Spanish
Sport	PE
Turnen	gymnastics

Meinungen	**Opinions**
Wie findest du (Mathe)?	What do you think of (maths)?
Ich finde (Mathe) toll.	I think (maths) is great.
Ich finde (Mathe) nicht toll.	I don't think (maths) is great.
Magst du (Kunst)?	Do you like (art)?
Ich mag (Kunst).	I like (art).
Ich mag (Kunst) nicht.	I don't like (art).
Was ist dein Lieblingsfach?	What's your favourite subject?
Mein Lieblingsfach ist (Sport).	My favourite subject is (sport).
einfach	easy

interessant	interesting
fantastisch	fantastic
furchtbar	awful
gut	good
langweilig	boring
prima	fabulous
doof	stupid
schwer	difficult
super	super

Wie spät ist es?	**What time is it?**
Es ist …	It is …
neun Uhr	nine o'clock
halb neun	half past eight
Viertel vor neun	quarter to nine
Viertel nach neun	quarter past nine
Mittag	12 o'clock (noon)
Mitternacht	12 o'clock (midnight)

Wann haben wir Mathe?	**When do we have maths?**
Um wie viel Uhr beginnt Kunst?	At what time does art begin?
Wir haben um zehn Uhr Mathe.	We have maths at ten o'clock.
Kunst beginnt um halb zwölf.	Art begins at half past eleven.

Wochentage	**Days of the week**
Montag	Monday
Dienstag	Tuesday
Mittwoch	Wednesday
Donnerstag	Thursday
Freitag	Friday
Samstag	Saturday
Sonntag	Sunday

Checklist

How well do you think you can do the following? Write a sentence for each one if you can.	I can do this well	I can do this but not very well	I can't do this yet
1 say what's in your classroom and your schoolbag			
2 use der/die/das and einen/eine/ein correctly			
3 say which school subjects you have			
4 give your opinion on school subjects			
5 tell the time			
6 say the days of the week			

1 🎧 **Listen to these people saying what hobbies they have. Work out who is who and write sentences.**

a

Sophie spielt Fußball.

e

_____

i

_____

b

_____

f

_____

j

_____

c

_____

g

_____

Arzu	Lukas
Carsten	Marie
Dennis	Rebecca
Heino	Sophie
Jessica	Tim

d

_____

h

_____

2 **Read this paragraph. Tick the sentences that are _richtig_ (true) and put a cross by the ones that are _falsch_ (false).**

> Hi! Ich heiße Marko. Ich spiele sehr gern Gitarre. Ich bin in einer Band. Ich spiele auch gern Schlagzeug, aber nicht so gut. Ich bin absolut nicht sportlich. Ich spiele nicht gern Tennis und ich spiele auch nicht gern Fußball. Meine Schwester Hilke ist sportlich, aber nicht musikalisch. Sie spielt gern Federball, aber nicht gern Geige!

a ✓ Marko likes playing guitar.

b ☐ He doesn't like playing the drums.

c ☐ He isn't sporty.

d ☐ He plays in a band.

e ☐ Hilke is sporty.

f ☐ She likes to play the violin.

g ☐ She likes playing badminton.

h ☐ She's in a band.

1 **Unjumble these sentences and write them out correctly.**

a gehe Ich einkaufen gern

Ich gehe _____

b Ich Internet gern chatte im

_____

c höre Ich Musik gern

_____

d Rad gern fahre Ich

_____

e sehe Ich fern gern

_____

f gern lese Ich

_____

2 **Put ticks by each picture to show what Ali likes (✓), prefers (✓✓) and likes best (✓✓✓).**

a ✓✓✓

b

c

d

e

f

gern ✓, lieber ✓✓, am liebsten ✓✓✓

3 **Choose the correct verb form.**

a Ich ___fahre___ nicht gern Skateboard. (**fahren**)

b Er _____ gern Klavier. (**spielen**)

c Claudia _____ am liebsten Rap. (**hören**)

d Ich _____ gern Bücher. (**lesen**)

e Alfons _____ lieber ins Kino. (**gehen**)

f Du _____ nicht gern am Computer. (**spielen**)

2A.3 Ich liebe Computerspiele

1 Complete this advert for a *ZOOM* computer game. Write in the correct words.

Lernst du Deutsch?

Das **ZOOM-Spiel** ist _____cool_____ (*cool*)!

Es ist _____ (*funny*) und _____ (*exciting*).

Das **ZOOM-Spiel** ist nicht _____ (*boring*).

Findest du Deutsch _____ (*terrible*)?

Nicht mit **ZOOM**.

Es ist _____ (*super*) und auch _____ (*useful*).

> schrecklich   cool   spannend   super   lustig   nützlich   langweilig

2 🎧 What does this person think of each type of game?
Write the answer in German.

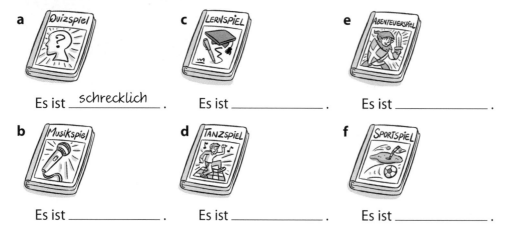

a Quizspiel
Es ist __schrecklich__ .

c Lernspiel
Es ist _____ .

e Abenteuerspiel
Es ist _____ .

b Musikspiel
Es ist _____ .

d Tanzspiel
Es ist _____ .

f Sportspiel
Es ist _____ .

3 Translate the second half of each sentence into German, using *denn*.

a Ich mag Sportspiele, __denn sie sind_____ .
(*because they are super*)

b Ich mag Lernspiele nicht, _____ .
(*because they are boring*)

c Ich mag Musikspiele, _____ .
(*because they are funny*)

d Ich mag Abenteuerspiele nicht, _____ .
(*because they are terrible*)

1 Find the correct expression for each picture and write the expression below each one.

a   b   c   d   e

am Montag _____ _____ _____ _____

am Abend   am Wochenende   am Nachmittag   am Montag   jeden Tag

2 🎧 Listen and write in below each picture, in English, when it is done.

a

every day _____

c

_____

e

_____

b

_____

d

_____

f

_____

3 Write four sentences saying what you do and how often.
They don't have to be true!

_____

_____

_____

_____

2A.5 Am Wochenende

1 **Draw lines to match the German and English expressions.**

am Wochenende	*every day*
am Mittwoch	*twice a week*
jede Woche	*on Wednesday*
am Abend	*at the weekend*
zweimal in der Woche	*every week*
jeden Tag	*in the evening*

2 **Write six sentences about yourself, using the time expressions above and vocabulary about activities you have learned in this unit.**

a Ich _____ jeden Tag _____ .

b Ich _____ .

c _____ .

d _____ .

e _____ .

f _____ .

3 **Read the paragraph and note down …**

- two things Claas is **positive** about and why.

  computer games – _____

  _____

- two things he is **negative** about and why.

  _____

  _____

Ich heiße Claas und ich wohne in Bremen in Norddeutschland. Ich spiele gern am Computer. Computerspiele sind spannend. Im Winter spiele ich Eishockey mit meinem Bruder. Das ist hart, aber sehr cool. Am Wochenende gehen wir oft einkaufen. Das finde ich nicht so gut. Es ist alles zu teuer. Fernsehen mag ich auch nicht, das finde ich langweilig.

ich spiele – du spielst – er/sie/es spielt – wir spielen – ihr spielt – sie/Sie spielen

1 Interpret the pictures and write sentences describing them.

a — Ich spiele Fußball.

b

c — ?

d — ?

e

f

2 Fill in the gaps.

	fahren – *to go*		**lesen** – *to read*
ich	fahre	ich	
du		du	
er / sie / es		er / sie / es	
wir		wir	
ihr		ihr	
sie / Sie		sie / Sie	

Positive or negative?

1 Write P (positive) or N (negative) by these words and expressions.

langweilig	N	schlecht		
gut		furchtbar		
super		lustig		
gern		prima		
nicht gern		nicht so gut		

> Words are often used to show what attitudes we have. Working out whether somebody's opinion of something is positive or negative can often help you a lot when you are trying to understand what somebody is saying to you, or in a listening exercise.

Syllables

2 Put together the syllables to make the German words for sports and musical instruments. Insert them in the grid and identify the shaded word. Each word has been started for you.

```
a  R U G [G]
b    T [E] N
c  K L A V
d    [G] I T
e  S C H W I M M
```

EN	BY	E
IER	NIS	ARR

The shaded word is _____ . It means _____ .

> German is a language where all the syllables in a word are pronounced. This makes reading simple because you just pronounce what you see on the page.

'e' at the end of a word

3 Translate these words into German and say them out loud. They all have an –e on the end.

snake, (I) drive, (I) play, (I) see, dogs, friends, (I) go, guitar

_____

P.S. In that list, can you spot …

- two singular nouns? _____
- two plural nouns? _____

> In English, an 'e' at the end of a word isn't normally pronounced (game, bottle, cassette). In German, you do pronounce it. It sounds a bit like 'uh'.

Ich spiele (nicht) gern ... — **I (don't) like playing ...**

Spielst du gern ...?	Do you like playing ...?
Basketball	basketball
Federball	badminton
Fußball	football
Rugby	rugby
Tennis	tennis
Volleyball	volleyball
Flöte	flute
Geige	violin
Gitarre	guitar
Klavier	piano
Schlagzeug	drums
am Computer	on the computer
in einer Band	in a band
Karten	cards
Schach	chess

Das mache ich am liebsten — **That's what I like doing most of all**

Ich besuche gern meine Freunde.	I like visiting my friends.
Ich chatte gern im Internet.	I like chatting on the internet.
Ich sehe gern fern.	I like watching TV.
Ich gehe gern ins Kino.	I like going to the cinema.
Ich gehe gern ins Café.	I like going to the café.
Ich gehe gern einkaufen.	I like going shopping.
Ich fahre gern Rad.	I like cycling.
Ich fahre gern Skateboard.	I like skateboarding.
Ich fahre gern Ski.	I like skiing.
Ich höre gern Musik.	I like listening to music.
Ich lese gern.	I like reading.
Ich tanze gern.	I like dancing.
Ich schwimme gern.	I like swimming.
Ich sehe lieber fern.	I prefer watching TV.
Ich spiele am liebsten Rugby.	Most of all I like playing rugby.
Ich sehe mir gern (Rugby) im Fernsehen an.	I like watching (rugby) on TV.

Ich liebe Computerspiele — **I love computer games**

das Abenteuerspiel	adventure game
das Lernspiel	educational game
das Musikspiel	music game
das Quizspiel	quiz game
das Sportspiel	sports game
das Tanzspiel	dance game
Magst du (Sportspiele)?	Do you like (sports games)?
Wie findest du (Quizspiele)?	How do you find (quiz games)?
Ich mag ... (nicht).	I (don't) like ...
..., denn ich finde sie ...	..., because I find them ...
anstrengend	tiring, strenuous
cool	cool
klasse	great

interessant	interesting
langweilig	boring
lustig	funny
nützlich	useful
schrecklich	awful, terrible
schwierig	difficult
spannend	exciting
toll	great

Wie oft machst du das? — **How often do you do that?**

am Montag, Dienstag, ...	on Monday, Tuesday, ...
am Wochenende	at the weekend
am Morgen	in the morning
am Nachmittag	in the afternoon
am Abend	in the evening
jeden Tag	every day
jeden Monat	every month
jede Woche	every week
jedes Jahr	every year
einmal/zweimal/dreimal in der Woche	once/twice/three times a week
Ich höre jeden Tag Musik.	I listen to music every day.

Checklist

How well do you think you can do the following?			
Write a sentence for each one if you can.			
	I can do this well	I can do this but not very well	I can't do this yet
1 say what your hobbies are (sport, music)			
2 use *gern*, *lieber*, *am liebsten*			
3 use irregular verbs like *lesen*, *sehen* and *fahren*			
4 give your opinions on hobbies			
5 use *denn* to mean because			
6 use expressions of time and frequency			

1 🎧 **Listen and write the names of the cities in the right places.**

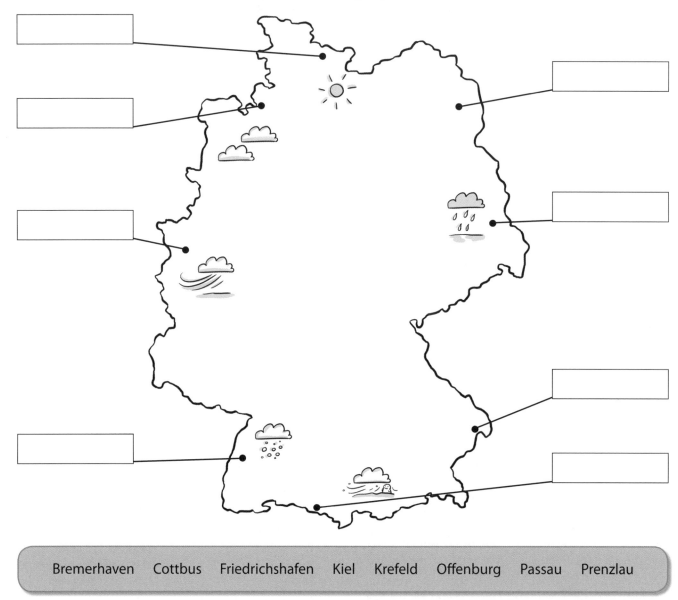

Bremerhaven   Cottbus   Friedrichshafen   Kiel   Krefeld   Offenburg   Passau   Prenzlau

2 **What's the weather like in these places? Write in the weather phrase.**

Im Norden: _Es ist sonnig._

Im Nordwesten: _____

Im Süden: _____

Im Westen: _____

Im Osten: _____

Im Südwesten: _____

Es schneit.
Es ist sonnig.
Es ist windig.
Es ist wolkig.
Es ist kalt.
Es regnet.

1 🎧 Listen to these people saying where they live. Write down, in English, where they live and what they think of it.

a   housing estate, _____

b   _____

c   _____

d   _____

2 Write down in English ...

a   where Anke lives   in the _____

b   whether she likes it   _____

c   four things she says about it   _____

                                               _____

> Ich heiße Anke. Ich wohne sehr gern auf dem Land. Es ist absolut nicht langweilig hier, es ist total cool! Es ist auch grün, das finde ich toll.

3 Like Anke, write a couple of lines about where you live and what you think of it.

_____

_____

_____

_____

2B.3 Mein Haus

1 🎧 Listen and write in the numbers.

a
__85__ Jahre alt

c
_____ Schüler

e
Nummer _____

g
Nummer _____

b
_____ €

d
_____ Bücher

f
_____ Bonbons

h
Größe _____

2 Now write out how each number in Activity 1 is spelled.

a __fünfundachtzig__   c _____   e _____   g _____

b _____   d _____   f _____   h _____

3 Solve the clues and fill in the crossword.

Waagerecht (across)

2 Where's my car?

4 Eat here

5 Oh Romeo!

7 Get wet here

8 Going underground

Senkrecht (down)

1 A room to get clean in.

3 For playing outside

6 What's cooking?

1 🎧 **Listen to Mirco describing his room. Fill in the answers in English, saying what is where.**

a The computer is ___on___ ___the___ ___desk___ .

b Mirco's clothes are _____ _____ _____ .

c The TV is _____ _____ _____ _____ .

d The cat is _____ _____ _____ .

e The chair is _____ _____ _____ _____ .

f The lamp is _____ _____ _____ ,

_____ the computer.

2 🎧 **Listen again and draw a sketch of Mirco's room.**

3 Using what you have learned on this spread, write a paragraph describing where the things in your bedroom are. Make sure you use the prepositions correctly.
Try to be adventurous and use new vocabulary. When you have looked up the genders of the words, you can apply the preposition rules.

_____

_____

_____

_____

_____

_____

_____

_____

1 🎧 **Listen to these numbers. Write down the numbers and also how they are spelled.**

a 55   *fünfundfünfzig*   d _____   g _____

b _____   e _____   h _____

c _____   f _____

2 **Complete these sentences describing where things are.**

Der Vogel sitzt ___*auf*___ dem Haus.   Die Garage ist _____ dem Haus.

Nils ist _____ Haus.   Das Rad ist _____ dem Haus.

Der Keller ist _____ dem Haus.

> im   neben
> hinter   vor   unter

3 **Write a few sentences describing what is in your room. Try to use new words, looking them up in a dictionary or online.**

_____

_____

_____

1 Translate these expressions into German, using *der* or *dem*.

After the prepositions *in, auf, hinter, neben, vor, unter, zwischen,* use
masculine   dem
feminine   der
neuter   dem

a on the table   auf dem Tisch

b under the chair   _____

c next to the cupboard   _____

d in the bag   _____

e in front of the school   _____

f behind the door   _____

g between the house and the garage

_____

h in front of the supermarket   _____

i in the car   _____

j in front of the post office   _____

der (m)	die (f)	das (n)
Tisch	Tasche	Haus
Stuhl	Schule	Auto
Schrank	Tür	
Supermarkt	Garage	
	Post	

2 Write in *einen, eine* or *ein*.

	masculine	feminine	neuter
Es gibt	einen	eine	ein

a In meiner Schule gibt es ___einen___ Schulhof.

b In meiner Schule gibt es _____ Bibliothek.

c In meinem Haus gibt es _____ Küche.

d In meinem Haus gibt es _____ Wohnzimmer.

e In meinem Haus gibt es _____ Badezimmer.

f In meiner Stadt gibt es _____ Supermarkt.

g In meiner Stadt gibt es _____ Kathedrale.

masculine	feminine	neuter
Schulhof	Bibliothek	Wohnzimmer
Supermarkt	Küche	Badezimmer
	Kathedrale	

1 🎧 Listen to the words. Put a tick if you hear the sound 'ch' and a cross if you don't.

a [✗]　c [ ]　　e [ ]　　g [ ]　　i [ ]
b [ ]　d [ ]　　f [ ]　　h [ ]　　j [ ]

2 🎧 Listen again and jot down the words as you go. Then say them out loud. Finally, check that you have spelled them correctly.

a _____　　f _____

b _____　　g _____

c _____　　h _____

d _____　　i _____

e _____　　j _____

3 Look back to the previous page (*Sprachlabor*). There are at least three nouns you haven't seen before but you can immediately work out what they mean. What are they?

_____

> Because German is so logical, and similar in many ways to English, it's often easy to work out meanings.

4 Practise using the correct words for 'a' in this sentence.

In meiner Tasche habe ich ____*eine*____ Zeitschrift,

_____ Buch, _____ Teddy, _____ Handy,

_____ DVD-Spieler, und _____ Maus!

masculine	feminine	neuter
DVD-Spieler	Zeitschrift	Handy
Teddy	Maus	Buch

> You can use correct articles even if you have never seen the words, as long as you know the gender. If the noun is masculine, use *einen*. If it's feminine, use *eine* and if it's neuter, use *ein*. Easy!

Adapting texts

5 You can now write substantial paragraphs using the models presented in the Student Book, and adapting them. Write a few lines describing your ideal home. There is space to write on page 80. Here is some vocabulary to help you.

> in den Bergen　am Meer　in der Stadt　auf dem Land
> (ziemlich) groß/klein/schön
> Es gibt ein Badezimmer / drei Schlafzimmer / ein Wohnzimmer

> P.S. It is very important to know genders in German. Always note the gender of any new noun you learn.

Meine Region	My region
im Norden	in the north
im Nordosten	in the north-east
im Nordwesten	in the north-west
im Osten	in the east
im Süden	in the south
im Südosten	in the south-east
im Südwesten	in the south-west
im Westen	in the west

Das Wetter	The weather
Es ist heiß/kalt.	It is hot/cold.
neblig, windig, wolkig	foggy, windy, cloudy
schön, sonnig, warm	nice, sunny, warm
Es friert.	It's freezing/It freezes.
Es gewittert.	There's thunder and lightning.
Es regnet.	It's raining/It rains.
Es schneit.	It's snowing/It snows.
Es (regnet) nicht.	It isn't (raining)/It doesn't (rain).

Wo wohnst du?	Where do you live?
ich wohne	I live
du wohnst	you live
er/sie wohnt	he/she lives
wir wohnen	we live
ihr wohnt	you live (plural)
sie wohnen	they live
Sie wohnen	you live (formal)
am Stadtrand	on the edge of town
auf dem Land	in the countryside
in der Stadt	in town
in einem Bungalow	in a bungalow
in einem Doppelhaus	in a semi-detached house
in einem Dorf	in a village
in einem Einfamilienhaus	in a detached house
in einem Haus	in a house
in einem Reihenhaus	in a terraced house
in einer Wohnsiedlung	on a housing estate
in einer Wohnung	in a flat

Wie ist es?	What is it like?
grün	green
interessant, langweilig	interesting, boring
laut	noisy, loud
praktisch	practical
schön, toll	beautiful, great

Mein Haus	My house
der Balkon	balcony
der Garten	garden
der Keller	cellar
die Dusche	shower
die Garage	garage
die Küche	kitchen

das Badezimmer	bathroom
das Esszimmer	dining room
das Schlafzimmer	bedroom
das Wohnzimmer	living room
im Erdgeschoss	on the ground floor
im ersten/zweiten Stock	on the first/second floor

Mein Zimmer	My room
In meinem Zimmer gibt es …	In my room there is …
einen Computer	a computer
einen Fernseher	a TV
einen Kleiderschrank	a wardrobe
einen Schreibtisch	a desk
einen Stuhl	a chair
eine Lampe	a lamp
eine Stereoanlage	a hi-fi system
ein Bett	a bed
ein Poster	a poster
ein Regal	a shelf
ein Sofa	a sofa
auf	on
hinter	behind
im	in the
neben	next to
unter	under
vor	in front of
zwischen	between

Zahlen	Numbers
zweiunddreißig	thirty-two
vierzig, fünfzig, sechzig	forty, fifty, sixty
siebzig, achtzig, neunzig	seventy, eighty, ninety
hundert	hundred

Checklist

How well do you think you can do the following? Write a sentence for each one if you can.	I can do this well	I can do this but not very well	I can't do this yet
1 say where you live			
2 say what the weather is like			
3 describe your house or flat			
4 say what's in your room			
5 count up to a hundred			
6 use auf, in, hinter, neben, vor, zwischen and unter correctly			

3A.1 Was isst du gern?

1 Write in the German words for the items.

a | Hähnchen

b |

c |

d |

e |

f |

g |

h |

i |

2 🎧 Listen to these people saying what they do and don't like to eat and drink. Write in the items in English.

a **Nils:** likes: _chicken,_____

doesn't like: _____

b **Susanne:** likes: _____

doesn't like: _____

3 Write out these sentences in the correct order.
Remember, the verb always comes second.

a Frühstück Zum esse Cornflakes ich

Zum Frühstück _____

b Banane Mittagessen esse Zum ich eine.

_____

c trinke Zum Wasser Abendessen ich.

_____

1 **Draw lines to show where you would buy these items.**

2 🎧 **Listen and work out where these people are.**
Write *PIZZERIA*, *EISDIELE*, *IMBISS* or *BÄCKEREI*.

a ___IMBISS___   d _____   g _____

b _____   e _____   h _____

c _____   f _____

3 🎧 **Listen again and write down, in English, what the people are ordering.**

a ___curried sausage with chips___   e _____

b _____   f _____

c _____   g _____

d _____   h _____

4 **Write down four orders for things you'd like to eat.**
Don't forget to be polite!

a Ich möchte _____ , bitte.

b _____

c _____

d _____

1 🎧 Listen to some large numbers. Write the numbers out in the order you hear them, first just the number, then the German word for it.

a <u>1000, tausend</u>

f _____

b _____

g _____

c _____

h _____

d _____

i _____

e _____

j _____

2 Write in the appropriate amounts.

a Ich möchte <u>einen Becher</u> Joghurt.

b Ich möchte _____ Cornflakes.

c Ich möchte _____ Cola.

d Ich möchte _____ Brötchen.

e Ich möchte _____ Milch.

f Ich möchte _____ Orangensaft.

> einen Liter   eine Tüte   eine Flasche
> eine Packung   eine Flasche   einen Becher

3 Make a shopping list with these items. Don't forget to include the amounts.

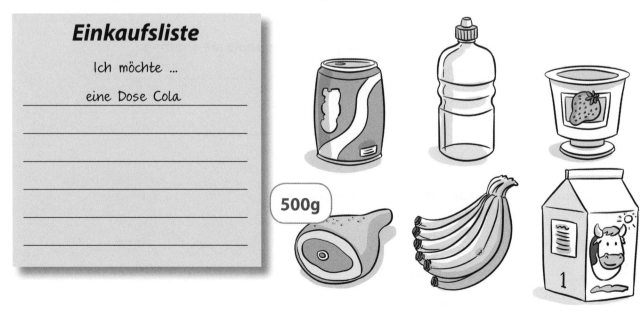

Einkaufsliste

Ich möchte ...

eine Dose Cola

_____

_____

_____

_____

_____

500g

3A.4 Ich esse kein Fleisch

1 **Herr Gierig and Frau Gierig have completely opposite tastes. Complete the sentences using *keinen*, *keine* or *kein*.**

Herr Gierig: Ich esse gern Bonbons.

Frau Gierig: _Und ich esse keine Bonbons._

Herr Gierig: Ich esse gern Schokolade.

Frau Gierig: _____

Herr Gierig: Ich esse gern Pommes.

Frau Gierig: _____

Herr Gierig: Ich esse gern Fleisch.

Frau Gierig: _____

Herr Gierig: Ich esse gern Apfelkuchen.

Frau Gierig: _____

Herr Gierig: Ich trinke gern Cola.

Frau Gierig: _____

masculine	Apfelkuchen
feminine	Schokolade, Cola
neuter	Fleisch
plural	Pommes, Bonbons

2 🎧 **Listen to these people and write, in English, what they don't eat and why.**

What?	Why?
a _fish_	_____
b _____	_____
c _____	_____
d _____	_____
e _____	_____

3 **Look at Activity 1 again. Give Herr Gierig some good health advice, using *Man soll …* and *keinen/keine/kein*. Go through all the things he eats and drinks.**

a _Man soll keine Bonbons essen._

b _____

c _____

d _____

e _____

f _____

4 **Now also say in each case what Herr Gierig _should_ be eating and drinking. Choose healthy items from this unit.**

a _Man soll jeden Tag Gemüse essen._

b _____

c _____

d _____

e _____

f _____

1 Work out the items and amounts. Complete the shopping list in German.

eine Dose	Erdbeermarmelade
sechs Scheiben	Kartoffeln
eine Flasche	Suppe
ein Becher	Chips
eine Packung	Mineralwasser
ein Glas	Joghurt
2 Kilo	Schinken

Einkaufsliste

ein Glas Erdbeermarmelade

_____

_____

_____

_____

_____

_____

2 Write sentences to show these people's opinions of food.

a   Ich esse gern Bratwurst. _____

b   _____

c   _____

d   _____

e   _____

f   _____

Ich esse gern / nicht gern …
Ich esse keinen / keine / kein …

3 🎧 Listen to the interview. Make notes and write a few sentences in English about Lukas' eating and drinking habits.

_____

_____

_____

4 🎧 Listen again and note down the interviewer's three questions. Then ask a partner those questions. In your conversation, include …

- three meals
- reasons
- linking words.

1 Unjumble these sentences and write the words out in the correct order. Always start with the meal. Remember, the verb is always the second piece of information.

a Cornflakes Zum esse Frühstück ich. _Zum Frühstück esse ich Cornflakes._

b Abendessen Brot esse Zum ich. _____

c Kaffee ich Zum trinke Frühstück. _____

d Mittagessen ich Zum esse Salat. _____

e Wasser Zum trinke Abendessen ich. _____

f trinke Mittagessen Zum Orangensaft ich.

_____

2 Tell these people off for their bad habits. Use *man soll* and *keinen*, *keine* or *kein*. If you are unsure about genders, look them up.

a Ich esse gern Bratwurst. _Man soll keine Bratwurst essen._

b Ich spiele gern Computerspiele. _____

c Ich trinke gern Whisky. _____

d Ich fahre gern Motorrad. _____

e Ich esse gern Schokolade. _____

f Ich trinke gern Bier. _____

3 Translate these sentences into English. They all contain linking words meaning 'and', 'or', 'but' or 'because'.

a Ich esse keinen Fisch, denn ich finde Fisch furchtbar. _I don't eat fish because I think fish is horrible._

b Ich spiele Hockey und ich spiele auch Tennis. _____

c Ich esse gern Salat, aber ich esse nicht gern Fleisch. _____

d Spielen wir am Computer oder gehen wir essen? _____

e Opa fährt nach Frankreich oder nach Schweden. _____

f Sonja mag gern Physik und Chemie. _____

g Olaf mag gern Chemie, aber nicht Physik. _____

h Wir lernen gern Deutsch, denn es macht Spaß. _____

Linking words

1 **What words should link these sentences?**

a Möchtest du Reis _____ Nudeln?

b Wir mögen Musik _____ Kunst.

c Ich möchte Bratwurst _____ keine Pommes.

d Ich spiele gut Fußball _____ nicht so gut Tennis.

e Ich schwimme gern, _____ ich bin sportlich.

f Wir mögen Cola, _____ es ist besser als Wasser.

g Ich trinke Kaffee _____ Tee.

h Möchtest du Käse _____ Wurst?

> To make your language sound more natural and less simple, try to use words to link sentences together. In this unit, four linking words are used. Can you remember them?

Pronunciation

2 **Say these words out loud and put them into the correct column.**

> Nudeln   Hund   Schule   du   Mutter   Joghurt   zum
> Butter   Erdkunde   Musik   Kunst   Bruder   Stuhl   Bus

> The vowel 'u' is pronounced in two different ways, as a 'short' vowel or a 'long' vowel.

short 'u'

Hund _____   _____

_____   _____

_____   _____

_____

long 'u'

Nudeln _____   _____

_____   _____

_____   _____

_____

Politeness

3 **Put these words into the correct column.**

> Ein Eis!   Ich möchte ein Eis, bitte!   Nein.   Ja.   Ja, bitte.   Nein, danke.
> Ein Eis, bitte.   Bitte schön.   Danke schön.   Ja?   Hier!

> In German, it is very important to be polite. This means saying *ich möchte* … rather than just saying the word, and using *bitte* and *danke* (just like in English!).

polite

Ich möchte ein Eis, bitte! _____

_____

_____

_____

_____

not so polite

Ein Eis! _____

_____

_____

_____

Essen und Trinken	**Food and drink**
Was isst du gern/nicht gern?	What do/don't you like eating?
Ich esse gern/nicht gern …	I like/don't like eating …
Brot	bread
ein Ei	an egg
eine Banane, einen Apfel	a banana, an apple
Fisch	fish
Hähnchen	chicken
Joghurt	yoghurt
Kartoffeln	potatoes
Käse	cheese
Nudeln	pasta
Reis	rice
Salat	salad
Was trinkst du gern/nicht gern?	What do/don't you like drinking?
Ich trinke gern/nicht gern …	I like/don't like drinking …
Cola	cola
Milch	milk
Orangensaft	orange juice

Mahlzeiten	**Meals**
Was isst/trinkst du …	What do you eat/drink …
zum Frühstück?	for breakfast?
zum Mittagessen?	for lunch?
zum Abendessen?	for dinner?
Zum Frühstück esse ich …	For breakfast I eat …
Zum Mittagessen trinke ich …	For lunch I drink …
Zum Abendessen …	For dinner …
Butter	butter
Cornflakes	cornflakes
Müsli	muesli
Marmelade	jam
Kaffee, Tee, Wasser	coffee, tea, water
meistens	mostly
normalerweise	usually

Etwas zu essen	**Ordering food**
Was darf es sein?	What would you like?
Was möchtest du?	What would you like?
Ja bitte?	Yes, please?
Kann ich Ihnen helfen?	Can I help you?
Ich möchte/nehme …, bitte.	I'd like …, please.
ein Erdbeereis	a strawberry ice cream
ein Schokoladeneis	a chocolate ice cream
ein Vanilleeis	a vanilla ice cream
mit/ohne Sahne	with/without cream
Pizza mit …	pizza with …
Oliven/Pilzen/Spinat	olives/mushrooms/spinach
Thunfisch/Tomaten/Zwiebeln	tuna/tomatoes/onions
Apfelkuchen	apple cake
Bio-Brot	organic bread
Bratwurst	fried sausage

Brötchen	bread rolls
Currywurst	curried sausage
Hamburger	hamburger
mit Mayonnaise/Ketchup	with mayonnaise/ketchup
Pommes frites	fries
Schwarzwälder Kirschtorte	Black Forest gateau

Im Geschäft	**In the shop**
Sonst noch etwas?	Anything else?
Nein danke, das ist alles.	No thanks, that's all.
250 Gramm	250 grams
ein (halbes) Pfund	(half) a pound
ein (halbes) Kilo	(half) a kilo
ein Glas Marmelade	a jar of jam
ein Stück Käse	a piece of cheese
eine Dose Cola	a can of cola
eine Flasche Wasser	a bottle of water
eine Packung Kaffee	a packet of coffee
eine Scheibe Schinken	a slice of ham
eine Tüte Brötchen	a bag of bread rolls
einen Becher Joghurt	a pot of yoghurt
einen Liter Milch	a litre of milk

Ich esse kein Fleisch	**I don't eat meat**
Man soll … essen/trinken.	You should eat/drink …
Man soll keinen/keine/kein … essen/trinken.	You shouldn't eat/drink …
Chips	crisps
Fastfood	fast food
Fleisch	meat
Gemüse	vegetables
Kuchen	cake
Obst	fruit
Schokolade	chocolate

Checklist

How well do you think you can do the following?			
Write a sentence for each one if you can.			
	I can do this well	I can do this but not very well	I can't do this yet
1 say what you like and don't like to eat and drink			
2 order food at a food stall			
3 buy food in a shop			
4 say how much you'd like			
5 count up to 1000			
6 use *sollen* correctly			

1 Solve the clues and fill in the crossword.

Waagerecht (across)
1 A place to do the weekly shopping
4 A place to buy stamps
6 Wet and wild
8 Good for a football match
9 A place to worship
10 Full of animals

Senkrecht (down)
1 A big, ancient building
2 A place for grass and trees
3 You can see a film here
5 A place to catch a train
7 Full of old things

Bahnhof   Kino
Kirche   Museum
Post   Park   Schloss
Schwimmbad   Stadion
Supermarkt   Zoo

Stadtpuzzle

2 🎧 Put numbers in the boxes to show the order in which you hear the places mentioned. Anything not mentioned, leave blank.

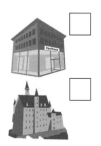

3 🎧 Listen again and note down, in English, at least three opinions expressed by the speaker.

4 Write in *einen*, *eine* or *ein*.

a Es gibt __einen__ Park.

b Es gibt _____ Kaufhaus.

c Es gibt _____ Kirche.

d Es gibt _____ Supermarkt.

e Es gibt _____ Kino.

f Es gibt _____ Bahnhof.

masculine	feminine	neuter
Park	Kirche	Kaufhaus
Supermarkt		Kino
Bahnhof		

1   **Identify the places and write in the word.**

1 PIZZERIA   3 JUGEND-ZENTRUM   5 SCHWIMMBAD   7 DISCO

2 STADION   4 CAFÉ   6 SKATEBOARD-BAHN   8 KINO

a   Man kann hier Freunde treffen. _Jugendzentrum_   e   Man kann hier Fußball spielen. _____

b   Man kann hier Kaffee trinken. _____   f   Man kann hier einen Film sehen. _____

c   Man kann hier tanzen. _____   g   Man kann hier schwimmen. _____

d   Man kann hier Pizza essen. _____   h   Man kann hier Skateboard fahren. _____

2   **Listen to Claudia describing Schwerin. Answer the questions in English.**

a   What's the first thing Claudia says about Schwerin?   _It's great._

b   What two places does she mention next? _____

c   What can you do in the park? _____

d   What can't you do there? _____

e   How many cinemas are there? _____

f   Is it a good place for eating out? _____

g   Where is Schwerin? _____

3   **Write sentences to fit the pictures.**

a   _Es gibt ein Restaurant. Man kann hier essen._

b   _____

c   _____

d   _____

e   _____

> Löwen sehen
> Englisch lernen
> ein Restaurant
> ein Kino
> Fußball spielen
> einen Park
> essen
> eine Schule
> einen Film sehen
> einen Zoo

3B.3 Wo ist das Kino?

1 Write the correct phrases below the pictures.

a

geradeaus

b

_____

c

_____

d

_____

e

_____

f

_____

g

_____

h

_____

> rechts   links   geradeaus   auf der linken Seite   auf der rechten Seite
> die erste Straße rechts   die zweite Straße links   die dritte Straße rechts

2 🎧 Use the pictures in Activity 1 again. Listen and write in the letters for the instructions given (2 letters each time).

a _a,_____   c _____   e _____   g _____

b _____   d _____   f _____   h _____

3 Write out the questions and answers.

a Wo ist der Bahnhof?

Nehmen Sie die erste Straße links.

b _____

_____

c _____

_____

d _____

_____

e _____

_____

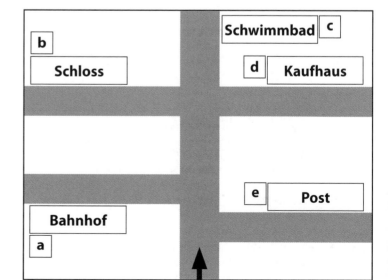

1 **Add the right captions to the pictures.**

a  zwei Erwachsene und ein Kind _____

b _____

c _____

d _____

e _____

f _____

> drei Karten   zwei Kinder   zwei Erwachsene und ein Kind
> vier Kinder   zwei Karten   drei Erwachsene

2 **What do these people want? Write the answers in English.**

a _a book_____

b _____

c _____

d _____

e _____

f _____

3 **Listen to Activity 2 again and turn the statements into questions.**

a _Möchtest du ein Buch?_____

b _____

c _____

d _____

e _____

f _____

1 Write sentences saying what things do and don't exist in this village.
Mention: a department store, a supermarket, a church, a castle,
a skateboard track, a train station and a TV tower.

Was gibt es in Dösdorf?

a _Es gibt kein Kaufhaus._

b _____

c _____

d _____

e _____

f _____

g _____

2 🎧 Listen to Ergül talking about Delmenhorst, the town where he lives.
Answer the questions in English.

a Where is Delmenhorst? _in North Germany_

b What does he say about swimming? _____

c What can he do at weekends? _____

d Can he go to the cinema in Delmenhorst? _____

e What can he do if he wants to watch football? _____

3 Write the instructions next to each picture.

a _Nehmen Sie die dritte Straße links._

b _____

c _____

d _____

e _____

f _____

Nehmen Sie …
　die erste / zweite / dritte Straße
　　links / rechts.
Gehen Sie geradeaus.
Gehen Sie links / rechts.

können / wollen

1 **Insert the correct form of *können* or *wollen*.**

a Ich _____kann_____ (*can*) schwimmen.

b Er _____ (*wants to*) Eis essen.

c Wir _____ (*can*) Deutsch sprechen.

d Roberta _____ (*can*) Gitarre spielen.

e _____ (*want to*) du ins Kino gehen?

f Mutti und Vati _____ (*want to*) nach Kiel fahren.

	können	**wollen**
ich	kann	will
du	kannst	willst
er/sie/es	kann	will
wir	können	wollen
ihr	könnt	wollt
sie/Sie	können	wollen

Instructions

2 **Fill in the gaps in these instructions.**

a ___Gehen Sie___ geradeaus. (*go – to an adult you don't know*)

b _____ keine Pommes. (*eat – to a friend*)

c _____ die erste Straße links. (*take – to a friend*)

d _____ mit dem Rad. (*travel – to an adult you don't know*)

e _____ nach Berlin. (*come – to an adult you don't know*)

f _____ ein Geschenk. (*buy – to a friend*)

Pronunciation

3 🎧 **Say these words out loud. Some you know, some you will have to work out. Then listen to the recording to check you got them right.**

Achterbahn	will	wild	voll	sprechen
schwimmen	wohne	wollen	besuchen	
möchte	Schloss	Weimar	vielleicht	bevor

Sentence patterns

1 Insert the correct sentence beginnings from the box below.

a __Kommen Sie__ nach <u>Soltau</u>!

b _____ <u>den Heide-Park</u>!

c _____ <u>Karussell</u>!

d _____ <u>Zuckerwatte</u>*!

e _____ <u>Souvenirs</u>!

f _____ <u>viele Attraktionen</u>.

g _____ <u>viel für Kinder</u>.

h _____ <u>Achterbahn</u>* fahren.

i _____ <u>Krokodile</u> sehen.

Man kann
Kommen Sie
Kaufen Sie
Man kann
Besuchen Sie
Essen Sie
Es gibt
Fahren Sie
Es gibt

* Zuckerwatte
– candy floss
* Achterbahn
– roller coaster

Looking at the structure of sentences can give you clues as to what they are saying. In this unit we had:
- sentences which are invitations (*Kommen Sie …! Besuchen Sie …!*)
- sentences saying what you can do (*Man kann …*)
- sentences saying what there is (*Es gibt …*).

2 How many sentences in the advert …

a invite you to do something? _____

b tell you what there is? _____

c tell you what you can do? _____

Adapting texts

3 Read the advert again. Write an advert for a different place. Use the sentences in the advert and change the details to those below.

_____

_____

_____

_____

_____

_____

It is easy to create your own texts by adapting existing ones and changing some of the content.

Worpswede   die Galerien   Bimmelbahn*   Aal*
Postkarten   alte Häuser   Pferdekutsche*   Künstler

* Bimmelbahn
– little train
* Aal – eel
* Pferdekutsche
– horse and carriage

4 Adapt the advert again to make an advert for your own town. Unsure of any vocabulary? Look it up in the dictionary!

Was gibt es? — What is there?

Es gibt (keinen/keine/kein) …	There is (no) …/There are (no) …
Gibt es …?	Is there …?
einen Bahnhof	a railway station
einen Fernsehturm	a TV tower
ein Geschäft	a shop
ein Jugendzentrum	a youth centre
ein Kaufhaus	a department store
ein Kino	a cinema
eine Kirche	a church
ein Museum	a museum
einen Park	a park
ein Schloss	a castle
ein Schwimmbad	a swimming pool
ein Stadion	a stadium
einen Supermarkt	a supermarket
eine Post	a post office
eine Skateboard-Bahn	a skatepark
eine U-Bahn-Station	an underground station
einen Zoo	a zoo

Was kann man machen? — What can one do?

Man kann (nicht) …	One can (not) …
Ich kann …	I can …
Kannst du …?	Can you …?
Freunde treffen	meet friends
Fußball spielen	play football
in der Disco tanzen	dance in the disco
ins Kino gehen	go to the cinema
ins Theater gehen	go to the theatre
Kaffee trinken	drink coffee
Pizza essen	eat pizza
Rad fahren	cycle
schwimmen	swim

Wo ist …? — Where is …?

der Bahnhof	the railway station
der Park	the park
die Post	the post office
das Schloss	the castle
das Schwimmbad	the swimming pool
die Skateboard-Bahn	the skatepark
das Stadion	the stadium
der Supermarkt	the supermarket

Richtungen — Directions

Geh …	Go … (informal)
Gehen Sie …	Go … (formal)
Nimm …	Take … (informal)
Nehmen Sie …	Take … (formal)
links	left
rechts	right
geradeaus	straight on

die erste Straße	the first road
die zweite Straße	the second road
die dritte Straße	the third road
über die Ampel	over the traffic lights
über die Kreuzung	over the crossing
über die Brücke	over the bridge
auf der linken Seite	on the left-hand side
auf der rechten Seite	on the right-hand side

Im Zoo — At the zoo

Ich möchte …	I'd like …
eine Karte	a ticket
zwei Karten	two tickets
für ein Kind	for a child
für zwei Kinder	for two children
für einen Erwachsenen	for an adult
für zwei Erwachsene	for two adults
Was kostet das?	How much does it cost?
Das kostet …	That costs …
Danke (schön).	Thank you.
Bitte (schön).	You're welcome.

Im Souvenirladen — In the souvenir shop

der Lolli	lollipop
das Notizbuch	notebook
die Plastikschlange	plastic snake
der Schlüsselanhänger	key ring
die Schneekugel	snow globe
die Schachtel Schokolade	box of chocolates
Ich suche …	I am looking for …
ein Geschenk	a present
Ich kaufe einen/eine/ein …	I (will) buy a …
Ich nehme einen/eine/ein …	I (will) take a …
Ich möchte einen/eine/ein …	I would like a …

Checklist

How well do you think you can do the following?			
Write a sentence for each one if you can.			
	I can do this well	I can do this but not very well	I can't do this yet
1 say what there is in a town			
2 say what you can do in a town			
3 give opinions about places			
4 ask for and give directions			
5 buy tickets and presents			
6 ask questions using verbs			

1 Find ten words for clothes in the grid and write them below. They can be across, down or diagonal.

J	L	B	A	L	L	E	R	I	N	A	S
H	E	M	D	D	I	F	B	S	M	E	P
U	D	A	B	E	S	T	O	K	I	F	O
L	E	O	N	W	Z	H	M	A	G	G	R
L	R	V	D	S	P	A	N	T	K	H	T
A	J	E	K	E	G	N	V	S	Z	P	S
Z	A	R	T	S	H	I	R	T	R	O	C
S	C	U	S	C	H	D	T	I	S	R	H
O	K	P	U	L	L	O	V	E	R	T	U
S	E	D	L	P	Z	N	Z	F	T	V	H
C	K	H	J	B	L	U	S	E	G	W	E
K	E	N	B	U	D	E	K	L	E	I	D

_____

_____

_____

_____

_____

_____

_____

_____

_____

_____

2 🎧 Listen to the adjectives and write in the letter of each one by the appropriate picture.

1 ☐ 2 ☐ 3 ☐ 4 ☐

5 [a] 6 ☐ 7 ☐ 8 ☐

3 Write in *ist* or *sind*.

a Der Pullover _____ zu klein.

b Die Jeans _____ schick.

c Die Stiefel _____ teuer.

d Die Shorts _____ hässlich.

e Der Mantel _____ zu lang.

f Die Sportschuhe _____ unbequem.

1 Read the article and work out who is who. Write the names in the blanks.

Aischa

SUPER-GIRLS

Wir präsentieren die 'Super-Girls', eine tolle neue Band aus Augsburg. **Jennifer** trägt einen weißen Kapuzenpullover und blaue Shorts. **Maike** trägt eine coole Hose und eine modische Jacke. **Aischa** trägt eine schwarze Jeans und ein rotes T-Shirt. **Fatima** trägt einen schönen Rock und eine gelbe Bluse.

2 Read the article again and describe in detail what each girl is wearing.

a Jennifer's hoodie is white and her _____

b _____

c _____

d _____

3 Complete the sentences.

a Ich möchte _____einen lässigen Rock_____ kaufen. (*casual skirt*)

b Ich möchte _____ tragen. (*comfortable jeans*)

c Ich möchte _____ kaufen. (*cheap shirt*)

d Ich möchte _____ haben. (*fashionable jacket*)

e Ich möchte _____ tragen. (*red pullover*)

masculine	feminine	neuter
einen …en	eine …e	ein …es

masculine	feminine	neuter
Rock	Jeans	Hemd
Pullover	Jacke	

1 🎧 **Listen to the conversation and answer the questions in English.**

a What item is mentioned first?   _A shirt._

b What is it like?   _____

c Does the girl like it?   _____

d What does she want to do?   _____

e What does the boy think?   _____

f What does he prefer?   _____

g What does the girl think of that?   _____

h What does she want to do?   _____

i What does the boy want to do?   _____

j Why?   _____

2 **Write in *ihn*, *sie* or *es*.**

a Die kurze Hose ist super. Ich möchte ____*sie*____ kaufen.

b Robbie Williams ist doof. Wir finden _____ nicht gut.

c Der Mantel ist zu groß. Sascha möchte _____ nicht kaufen.

d Das Kleid ist toll. Ich kaufe _____ .

e Ich mag Madonna gern. Wie findest du _____ ?

f Die Hose ist teuer, aber Ulli möchte _____ anprobieren.

3 **Translate these sentences to make a conversation in a clothes shop.**
Note: the shop assistant is an adult and the customer is a child.

a Can I help you?   _Kann ich dir helfen?_

b I like the red skirt.   _____

c Would you like to try it on?   _____

d Yes, please.   _____

e How do you find it?   _____

f I think it's good.   _____

g Would you like to buy it?   _____

h Yes, I'll buy it.   _____

1 **Write two sentences about each pair of pictures, using comparative adjectives.**

a Die Stiefel sind ___teurer___ als die Schuhe.

Die Schuhe sind _____ als die Stiefel.

b _____

_____

c _____

_____

d _____

_____

> groß   schön   billig   klein
> teuer   neu   hässlich   alt
> die Maus   der Elefant   das Auto
> das Motorrad   die Königin   das Monster

2 **Make these sentences future.**

a Ich fahre nach Berlin.

_Ich werde nach Berlin fahren._____

b Wir gehen zu H&M.

_____

c Ali kauft eine Jeans.

_____

d Wir essen Pommes.

_____

e Ich spiele Tischtennis.

_____

3 🎧 **Listen to each sentence. Write 'P' if it is present and 'F' if it is future.**

a ☐ P   **b** ☐   **c** ☐   **d** ☐   **e** ☐   **f** ☐

1 **Translate these words.**

nice ___schön___

boring _____

more boring _____

cheaper _____

uglier _____

nicer _____

more interesting _____

cheap _____

more modern _____

interesting _____

old _____

modern _____

ugly _____

older _____

hässlich

alt

2 🎧 **Listen to Tanja and answer the questions.**

a When is Tanja going shopping?

___On Saturday.___

b What's she going to buy? (2 things)

_____

c Why does she prefer H&M to Esprit? (2 reasons)

_____

d What else would she like to buy? (2 things)

_____

e What's the problem?

_____

4A.6A Sprachlabor

Direct object pronouns

1 **Write in *ihn*, *sie* or *es*.**

a Ich mag __ihn__ . (*jumper*)

b Wir finden _____ schön. (*shirt*)

c Ich trage _____ gern. (*school uniform*)

d Claudia möchte _____ kaufen. (*skirt*)

e Ich finde _____ zu teuer. (*computer*)

f Mehmet mag _____ gern. (*skateboard*)

g Ich möchte _____ anprobieren. (*jeans*)

h Wir essen _____ nicht gern. (*meat*)

masculine	feminine	neuter
Pullover	Schuluniform	Hemd
Rock	Jeans	Skateboard
Computer		Fleisch

der ...	→	ihn
die ...	→	sie
das ...	→	es

Adjective endings

2 **Write in the correct endings.**

Manja kauft einen gelb__en__ Mantel,

eine modisch____ Jacke,

ein lässig____ T-Shirt, einen warm____ Pullover

und billig____ Schuhe.

masculine	feminine	neuter	plural
einen ...en	eine ...e	ein ...es	...e

masculine	feminine	neuter	plural
Mantel	Jacke	T-Shirt	Schuhe
Pullover			

Manjas Einkaufsliste

Mantel (gelb)
Jacke (modisch)
T-Shirt (lässig)
Pullover (warm)
Schuhe (billig)

werden

3 **Write in the correct form of the verb *werden*.**

a Ich __werde__ diese Jacke nicht kaufen.

b _____ du schwimmen gehen?

c Gerd _____ Rad fahren.

d Ihr _____ im Imbiss essen.

e Wir _____ morgen Wii spielen.

f Meine Eltern _____ im Sommer nach England fahren.

False friends

1 These words look English but each has a different meaning in German. What are the meanings?

German word		English meaning
a Rock		_____
b Hose		_____
c rot		_____
d gut		_____
e elf		_____
f bin		_____
g hat		_____
h Tag		_____
i mag		_____
j links		_____

> It's surprising the number of German words which look like English ones but mean something completely different. Don't be deceived!

Pronunciation

2 Although the English and German words look the same, they sound different. Read the words in Activity 1 aloud twice, once using the English pronunciation and once using the German.

'Cognates'

3 Look carefully at these words and write C (Cognate) or NC (Near Cognate) by each word.

☐ Pullover ☐ Musik ☐ braun

☐ Jeans ☐ cool ☐ Spanisch

☐ T-Shirt ☐ intelligent ☐ Mathe

☐ Bluse ☐ Elefant ☐ Sport

☐ Party ☐ Banane ☐ Gitarre

> In contrast to 'false friends', 'cognate' words are words which look and mean the same in English and German. 'Near cognates' mean the same but are spelled slightly differently.

Die Jeans ist cool! — *Jeans are cool!*

die Ballerinas	*pumps/ballerina shoes*
die Bluse	*blouse*
das Hemd	*shirt*
die Hose	*trousers*
die Jeans	*jeans*
der Kapuzenpullover	*hoodie*
das Kleid	*dress*
die Kleidung	*clothes/clothing*
die Lederjacke	*leather jacket*
der Mantel	*coat*
der Pullover	*jumper*
der Rock	*skirt*
die Shorts	*shorts*
die Sportschuhe	*trainers*
die Stiefel	*boots*
das T-Shirt	*T-shirt*
alt	*old*
altmodisch	*old-fashioned*
bequem	*comfortable*
billig	*cheap*
bunt	*multicoloured*
gestreift	*stripy*
hässlich	*ugly*
kariert	*checked*
kurz	*short*
lässig	*casual*
modisch	*fashionable*
neu	*new*
schick	*chic/smart*
schön	*beautiful*
teuer	*expensive*
unbequem	*uncomfortable*
sehr	*very*
total	*totally*
ziemlich	*quite*

Coole Outfits — *Cool outfits*

Ich trage …	*I wear …*
Er/Sie trägt …	*He/She wears …*
… einen gelben Rock	*… a yellow skirt*
… ein teures Kleid	*… an expensive dress*
… eine schwarze Jacke	*… a black jacket*
… lässige Shorts	*… casual shorts*
normalerweise	*normally/usually*
Ich möchte … tragen.	*I'd like to wear …*
Ich möchte … kaufen.	*I'd like to buy …*
Ich möchte einkaufen gehen.	*I'd like to go shopping.*
Ich möchte schick aussehen.	*I'd like to look smart.*

Wir gehen einkaufen! — *We're going shopping!*

Wie findest du …?	*What do you think of …?*
Ich finde ihn/sie/es …	*I find it …*
Ich finde sie (pl) …	*I find them …*
zu groß/klein	*too big/small*
zu teuer	*too expensive*
Es steht dir gut.	*It suits you.*
Es steht dir nicht.	*It doesn't suit you.*
Wie kann ich dir helfen?	*How can I help you?*
Ich möchte (ihn) anprobieren.	*I'd like to try it on.*
Ich möchte (sie) kaufen.	*I'd like to buy it/them.*
Ich möchte (es) nicht kaufen.	*I wouldn't like to buy it.*

Die Hose ist zu klein! — *The trousers are too small!*

Mein Outfit ist zu alt.	*My outfit is too old.*
Ich werde einkaufen gehen.	*I'll go shopping.*
Ich werde … kaufen.	*I'll buy …*
Ich werde (ihn) umtauschen.	*I'll exchange it.*
Ich werde … tragen.	*I'll wear …*
eine Größe kleiner	*a size smaller*
eine Größe größer	*a size bigger*
besser (als)	*better (than)*

Das trage ich! — *That's what I wear!*

Was trägst du gern?	*What do you like wearing?*
Ich trage (am liebsten) …	*My favourite clothes are …*
Wo kaufst du ein?	*Where do you go shopping?*
Ich kaufe meine Kleidung bei …	*I buy my clothes at …*
Was trägst du in der Schule?	*What do you wear at school?*
In der Schule trage ich …	*At school I wear …*
die Schuluniform	*school uniform*
die Designerkleidung	*designer clothing*
die Krawatte	*tie*
hellblau	*light blue*

Checklist

How well do you think you can do the following? Write a sentence for each one if you can.	I can do this well	I can do this but not very well	I can't do this yet
1 talk about, compare and give opinions on clothes			
2 use the singular and plural forms of nouns followed by *ist* and *sind*			
3 use adjective endings in the accusative case			
4 use *ich möchte* correctly			
5 use the words for 'it' (*ihn/sie/es*) and 'them' (*sie*)			
6 use the future tense			

1 🎧 **Listen to the conversation and answer the questions in English.**

a Where is Olaf going on holiday? ___Spain_____

b How is he going to travel? _____

c What accommodation will he have? _____

d How long is he staying? _____

e What does he say about the weather
in Mallorca? _____

f Is he going on his own? _____

2 **Write in *einer* or *einem*.**

a Ich wohne in ___einem_____ Wohnwagen.

b Wir wohnen in _____ Jugendherberge.

c Ich wohne auf _____ Campingplatz.

d Jessica wohnt in _____ Wohnmobil.

e Mohammad wohnt in _____ Ferienwohnung.

f Ich wohne in _____ Ferienhaus.

masculine	feminine	neuter
Wohnwagen	Jugendherberge	Wohnmobil
Campingplatz	Ferienwohnung	Ferienhaus

	masculine	feminine	neuter
in	einem	einer	einem

3 **Fill in the grid in English.**

	Mode of transport	Where?
a	car	
b		
c		
d		

a Wir fahren mit dem Auto nach Italien.

b Ich fahre mit dem Zug nach Österreich.

c Ursel fliegt in die Türkei.

d Familie Müller fährt mit dem Wohnmobil nach Frankreich.

1 Complete the sentences in the same order as the places are mentioned in the brochure.

Hansestadt Hamburg

In Hamburg gibt es ...

- ➡ *einen Hafen*
- ➡ *einen Marktplatz*
- ➡ *viele Fischrestaurants*
- ➡ *einen Zoo (Hagenbecks Tierpark)*
- ➡ *den Dom (Freizeitpark)*
- ➡ *ein Schifffahrtsmuseum*

a Wir können ___eine Hafenrundfahrt machen.___

b Wir können _____

c Wir können _____.

d Wir können _____.

e Wir können _____.

f Wir können _____.

The *Dom* in Hamburg isn't a cathedral (the usual meaning of the word); it's a huge fairground.

You can work out the meaning of *Schifffahrtsmuseum* because it's made up of words you will recognise.

Fisch essen   ins Museum gehen   eine Hafenrundfahrt machen
Karussell fahren   zum Zoo gehen   auf dem Markt einkaufen

2 🎧 Listen to these people planning a day out in Hamburg. Write down, in English, ...

a three things the people will do _____

_____

_____

b two things they won't do, and why. _____

_____

1 🎧 **Listen to these people talking. Write Past, Present or Future and exactly where or when.**

a _future, tomorrow_

b _____

c _____

d _____

e _____

f _____

g _____

h _____

2 **Write in the correct form of *haben* or *sein*.**

a Wir __haben__ Tennis gespielt.

b Ich _____ nach Spanien gefahren.

c Wir _____ nach Frankfurt geflogen.

d Ich _____ in einem Hotel gewohnt.

e Wir _____ mit dem Zug gefahren.

f Wir _____ einen Ausflug gemacht.

> *fahren* and *fliegen* use *sein* in the perfect tense.

3 **Complete the sentences with the correct form of *haben* and the correct past participle.**

a Ich __habe__ eine Bratwurst __gekauft__ .

b Wir _____ Tennis _____ .

c Wir _____ eine Stadtrundfahrt _____ .

d Ich _____ Musik _____ .

| gemacht | gehört | gekauft | gespielt |

4B.4 Im Prater

1 **Write in the correct words.**

a Wir haben ___letztes___ ___Wochenende___ einen Ausflug nach Wien gemacht.
(*last weekend*)

b Ich werde _____ in der Disco tanzen. (*tomorrow*)

c Wir spielen _____ mit dem Computer. (*today*)

d Ich esse _____ _____ Cornflakes. (*every day*)

e Angela geht _____ _____ _____ schwimmen. (*twice a week*)

f Boris ist _____ ins Kino gegangen. (*yesterday*)

> gestern   heute   morgen   jeden Tag
> zweimal in der Woche   letztes Wochenende

2 🎧 **Listen to the phone conversation. Write Past, Present or Future, and exactly when.**

a travelling by underground train ___past, yesterday___

b playing cards _____

c going on fairground rides _____

d going to the cinema _____

e listening to music _____

f staying in _____

1 🎧 **Listen to these people talking about holidays. For each speaker, note down one thing they did in the past and one thing they will do in the future.**

a Past: _gone to England_

Future: _____

b Past: _____

Future: _____

c Past: _____

Future: _____

d Past: _____

Future: _____

2 **Read the text. Write down, in English …**

- three things Joachim has already done

_____

_____

_____

- three things he will do

_____

_____

_____

- at least four general facts (mentioned in the present tense)

_____

_____

_____

_____

Ich bin letzte Woche mit meiner Familie nach München gefahren. München ist eine tolle Stadt. Wir haben eine Stadtrundfahrt gemacht und ich habe ein neues T-Shirt gekauft. In München kann man gut essen und trinken. Das Bier ist billig, aber ich bin noch zu jung für Bier. Nächste Woche werden wir nach Innsbruck fahren. Das ist in Österreich. Wir werden Ski laufen und Snowboard fahren. Das Wetter in Österreich ist kalt im Winter.

Joachim

Perfect tense with *haben* or *sein*

1 Write in the correct form of *haben* or *sein* plus the correct past participle.

a Wir __haben__ Eis __gegessen__ . (*eaten*)

b Ich _____ eine Jacke _____ . (*bought*)

c Wir _____ in einem Hotel _____ . (*stayed*)

d Ich _____ Gitarre _____ . (*played*)

e Wir _____ in die Schule _____ . (*gone*)

f Ich _____ nach Italien _____ . (*travelled*)

g Wir _____ nach Amerika _____ . (*flown*)

h Ich _____ zum Imbiss _____ . (*gone*)

> Ich habe / bin …   + past participle
> Wir haben / sind …   at the end.

2 Fill in the gaps. Look back through this unit to find the information.

verb	past participle	*haben* or *sein*?
machen	_gemacht_	_haben_
hören	_____	_____
fahren	_____	_____
tanzen	_____	_____
gehen	_____	_____
essen	_____	_____
fliegen	_____	_____
kaufen	_____	_____
wohnen	_____	_____

> Not heard the word *Gasthaus* before? No problem. It's very similar to an English word, so you can work out the meaning. And you know its gender, so you can work out the dative. That's why German is so easy!

einem / einer

3 Fill in the gaps with *einem* or *einer*.

a auf _____ Campingplatz

b in _____ Hotel

c in _____ Jugendherberge

d in _____ Ferienwohnung

e in _____ Wohnwagen

f in _____ Gasthaus

masculine	feminine	neuter
Campingplatz	Jugendherberge	Hotel
Wohnwagen	Ferienwohnung	Gasthaus

masculine	feminine	neuter
einem	einer	einem

Compound nouns

1 **Find compound nouns meaning:**

a a hostel for youth   Jugendherberge

b a house for holidays   _____

c a place for camping   _____

d a car for living in   _____

e a park for free time   _____

f a journey round a town   _____

g a bath for swimming   _____

h a huge wheel   _____

i a cupboard for clothes   _____

j ice made with chocolate   _____

Schokoladeneis

Freizeitpark

Riesenrad

Stadtrundfahrt

Ferienhaus

Wohnwagen

Kleiderschrank

Jugendherberge

Schwimmbad

Campingplatz

It's fun to analyse the structure of words in German because so many words are constructed from putting together other words to make a new meaning. It also helps you to understand words which may seem new but are actually made out of words you already know.

Opinions

2 **Translate these opinions into German.**

a I'm looking forward to it.

   Ich freue mich darauf.

b I find that boring.

   _____

c I don't find that boring.

   _____

d That's great.

   _____

e I'm not looking forward to it.

   _____

f That pleases me.

   _____

g That's fun!

   _____

h That doesn't please me.

   _____

Expressing your opinions is important and it can also help you to reach a higher National Curriculum level in German. Examples of ways to give opinions are:
• using positive and negative adjectives
• *Ich finde …* (I think / find …)
• *Ich freue mich …* (I'm looking forward …)
• *Das gefällt mir.* (It pleases me / I like it.)

Here are some listening skills to take on to the next part of the course.
• Get clues from pictures and titles.
• Read the questions carefully.
• Anticipate probable answers and see if you are right.
• Listen to the tone of voice for clues.

Wohin fährst du in den Ferien?	*Where are you going on holiday?*	**Was werdet ihr machen?**	*What will you do?*
Ich fahre/Wir fahren …	*I am/We are going …*	Wir werden …	*We will …*
nach Frankreich	*to France*	(meine) Freunde treffen	*meet up with (my) friends*
nach Italien	*to Italy*	ein Eis kaufen	*buy an ice cream*
an die Nordsee	*to the North Sea*	ein Picknick machen	*go on a picnic*
in die Türkei	*to Turkey*	Pizza essen	*eat pizza*
		das Schloss Schönbrunn besuchen	*visit Schönbrunn Palace*
Wie fährst du?	*How are you travelling/ going?*	schwimmen	*go swimming*
Ich fahre/Wir fahren mit …	*I am/We are going by …*	Souvenirs kaufen	*buy souvenirs*
dem Auto	*car*	ins Theater gehen	*go to the theatre*
dem Wohnmobil	*camper van*		
dem Wohnwagen	*caravan*	**Was hast du gemacht?**	*What did you do?*
dem Zug	*train*	Wir haben/Ich habe …	*We/I …*
Ich fliege/Wir fliegen.	*I am/We are going by plane. I am/We are flying.*	einen Ausflug gemacht	*went on an excursion*
		in der Disco getanzt	*danced in the disco*
		Frisbee gespielt	*played frisbee*
Wo wohnst du?	*Where are you staying?*	Karten gekauft	*bought tickets*
Ich wohne/Wir wohnen …	*I am/We are staying …*	Musik im Park gehört	*listened to music in the park*
auf einem Campingplatz	*on a campsite*	Souvenirs gekauft	*bought souvenirs*
in einem Ferienhaus	*in a holiday home*		
in einer Ferienwohnung	*in a holiday apartment*	**Wohin bist du gefahren?**	*Where did you go?*
in einem Hotel	*in a hotel*	Ich bin/Wir sind …	*I/We …*
in einer Jugendherberge	*in a youth hostel*	nach Italien gefahren	*went to Italy*
in einem Wohnmobil	*in a camper van*	in die Türkei geflogen	*flew to Turkey*
in einem Wohnwagen	*in a caravan*	Wo hast du gewohnt?	*Where did you stay?*
in einem Zelt	*in a tent*	Ich habe/Wir haben in … gewohnt.	*I/We stayed in …*
Wie lange bleibst du/bleibt ihr dort?	*How long are you staying there?*		
Ich bleibe/Wir bleiben (eine Woche) dort.	*I am/We are staying there (a week).*		
zwei Wochen (lang)	*two weeks*		
eine Woche	*one week*		
zehn Tage	*ten days*		

Checklist

Was können wir machen?	*What can we do?*
Wir können/wollen …	*We can/want to …*
Ich kann/will …	*I can/want to …*
in einen Freizeitpark gehen	*go to an amusement park*
ins Museum gehen	*go to a museum*
mit dem Riesenrad fahren	*go on the Ferris wheel*
den Stephansdom besuchen	*visit St Stephan's Cathedral*
eine Stadtrundfahrt machen	*go on a tour of the town*
im Wasserpark spielen	*play in the waterpark*
ein Wiener Schnitzel essen	*eat a veal escalope*

How well do you think you can do the following?			
Write a sentence for each one if you can.			
	I can do this well	I can do this but not very well	I can't do this yet
1 say where you are going on holiday			
2 say how you are getting there			
3 say where you are staying and for how long			
4 describe a holiday in the past			
5 use modal verbs correctly			
6 use the perfect tense correctly			

Zoom in on your students' needs for KS3 German
with fully integrated video drama

Zoom Deutsch is an inspiring two-part German course offering fresh, exciting material and a fully integrated video drama for the whole ability range at Key Stage 3.

The course is flexible and relevant, taking account of the ever increasing diversity of students' abilities and language learning backgrounds. It is fully up-to-date and follows the renewed Key Stage 3 Framework for Languages and the revised Key Stage 3 Programme of Study.

This Workbook provides:

- differentiated practice material for the key language in each unit
- consolidation of key grammar points and language learning skills
- checklists and vocabulary lists for each unit so students can revise the language they've learnt and check their progress
- extra audio material for listening practice

Zoom Deutsch Student Book 1	978 0 19 912770 2
Zoom Deutsch Foundation Workbook 1	978 0 19 912810 5
Zoom Deutsch Higher Workbook 1	978 0 19 912811 2
Zoom Deutsch Teacher Book 1	978 0 19 912775 7
Zoom Deutsch Audio CDs 1	978 0 19 912773 3
Zoom Deutsch Interactive Oxbox 1	978 0 19 912776 4
Zoom Deutsch Assessment Oxbox 1	978 0 19 912777 1

OXFORD
UNIVERSITY PRESS

How to get in touch:
web www.oxfordsecondary.co.uk
email schools.enquiries.uk@oup.com
tel 01536 452620
fax 01865 313472

ISBN 978-0-19-912772-

9 780199 127726